TURNIP GREENS &

GRACE

A Story of Faith, Family, and the Fight of My Life

by Jerry M. Herrin

Turnip Greens & Grace

A Story of Faith, Family, and the Fight of My Life

Copyright © 2026 Grace & Iron Publishing

All rights reserved. No part of this book may be reproduced in any form or by an electronic or mechanical means, including information storage and retrieval systems, without permission in writing from the author, except by a reviewer who may quote brief passages in a review.

Disclaimer:

This book is a memoir. It reflects the author's present recollections of experiences over time. Some names and characteristics have been changed, some events have been compressed, and some dialogue has been recreated to protect the privacy of the individuals involved.

ISBN: 979-8-9945319-2-1

Printed in the United States of America

Scripture quotations are from the King James Version (KJV) of the Bible.

Dedication

For Stephanie,

whose love steadied my steps when I could barely stand.

For Bradley and Dawson,

who gave me every reason to fight and every reason to smile.

For my family,

who taught me the values of hard work, faith, and love that money could never buy.

And for every fighter who has faced a diagnosis, a setback, or a season of fear—may you be reminded that faith is stronger than fear, and grace is always within reach.

This book is for you.
May it remind you to live for today and find purpose in every breath.

"My grace is sufficient for thee, for my strength is made perfect in weakness." – 2 Corinthians 12:9 (KJV)

TABLE OF CONTENTS

Dedication
Preface: The Flavor of Resilience
Prologue: The Return

PART I: THE CLIMB
Chapter 1: Roots & Rules
Chapter 2: The Car Business & the "Old Dog"
Chapter 3: The Passover
Chapter 4: The Glass Office

PART II: THE BREAKING
Chapter 5: The First Fight
Chapter 6: The Call
Chapter 7: The Chair
Chapter 8: Steph's Song

PART III: THE BECOMING
Chapter 9: Surrender vs. Control
Chapter 10: Turnip Greens & the Lens of Gratitude
Chapter 11: The Limp: Second Chances
Chapter 12: Servant Leadership: The Business of People
Chapter 13: Trust Over Talent
Chapter 14: The Signature of God
Chapter 15: The Rules of the Road

Epilogue: The Golf Cart & the Next Chapter
Acknowledgments
About the Author

Preface/Introduction

Every person has a story, but not everyone slows down long enough to truly live it. For most of my life, that was me. I moved too fast to notice anything. I chased success at full sprint, long hours, long odds, and longer stretches of pretending that achievement equaled purpose. Somewhere beneath the noise and the striving were the real treasures: faith, family, and a quiet but steady grace I did not yet understand.

My journey has taken me to mountaintops and through deep valleys, across moments of triumph and moments when the ground felt like it was falling out from under me. I have heard God's whispers in the middle of chaos, felt his hand in the middle of uncertainty, and learned that sometimes the loudest lessons come in the softest ways.

This is not a story about the car business, though you will see where those long days and hard lessons shaped who I became. It is not a story about cancer, though the battle against Stage 4 renal cell carcinoma forever changed the course of my life. It is a story about how the blows meant to break you can become the very foundation on which you stand. It is a story about how God's grace does not just save but shapes, strengthens, and stretches you into someone new.

I started this journey as a nineteen-year-old kid selling cars in a small town, trying to figure out what success looked like. I climbed ladders, fell off, and learned through experience that leadership has nothing to do with titles and everything to do with people. Through every lesson earned and every painful moment, one truth rose above the rest: We do not walk alone.

When the doctor told me the cancer had returned, and spread, I thought my story was ending. God had already written a different chapter. He surrounded me with people who became lifelines: My wife whose strength carried mine, my family who held me up, my friends who prayed when I could not, and coworkers who rallied around me with loyalty I will never forget. Through them, I learned what it truly means to live with gratitude, courage, and grace.

This book is not about perfection. It is about perseverance. It is about the kind of faith that holds when nothing else does. It is about the moments that bring you to your knees and the grace that helps you stand back up.

Whether you're leading a team, leading a family, or simply trying to make it through another day, I hope these pages remind you of this simple truth: you are stronger than you think, loved more than you know, and carried by a God who does not waste a single moment of your story.

If you find echoes of your own journey in mine, I pray it gives you courage.

If you are walking through a trial, I pray it gives you hope. And if you have ever wondered whether faith still matters in this complicated world, this book is my answer: it absolutely does.

Turnip Greens & Grace offers lessons of faith, determination, and perseverance born from real-life challenges—for anyone feeling at their limit.

– Jerry M. Herrin Jr.

PROLOGUE

The Return

The sky was a blinding, indifferent shade of blue that mocks you when your world is falling apart. It was an ordinary Thursday in October. The kind of day where people worry about traffic on I-75, or what to make for dinner, or the email they forgot to send before leaving the office.

As Steph and I drove down the highway toward the doctor's office, I watched the cars passing us in the other lane. I saw a woman singing along to the radio, her head bobbing to a rhythm I could not hear. I saw a man drinking coffee, checking his watch, late for a meeting that felt important to him.

I felt a strange, sudden surge of envy. I envied their boredom. I envied their routine. I envied the luxury of their small, solvable problems. They were living in the world of the "normal," a world I had been exiled from the moment the phone rang earlier that morning.

It was a call from Amber, a nurse from my doctor's office. She was always kind, professional, and reassuring. This morning, her voice had been tight. There was no small talk about the weather or the upcoming holidays.

"Jerry," she had said. "The doctor wanted me to call you and ask if you could come see him today."

"Today?" I had asked, looking at my calendar, my mind automatically trying to reshuffle meetings and calls. "I am pretty booked. Can it wait until next week? I am open next week."

There was a pause on the other end of the line. A heavy, pregnant pause that lasted only a second but felt like an hour.

"No, Jerry," she said, and her voice dropped an octave, stripping away the pretense of negotiation. "He wants to see you *now*."

In the medical world, "now" is never good. "Now" is a terrifying word. "Now" means the shadow on the scan is not a shadow. "Now" means the plan has changed. "Now" means you need to stop driving the car of your life and hand over the keys, because you are no longer in control.

I hung up the phone and looked at Steph. She was standing in the kitchen, talking to a friend, the morning light catching her hair. When she saw my face, she stopped her conversation. She did not ask what happened. She just went to get her purse.

I said, "We need to go. That was Dr. Abdualla's office. He wants to see us right now."

I clenched my fists until my knuckles turned white. I tried to regulate my breathing, counting the mile markers as they blurred past. One. Two. Three. I tried to pray, but the words felt stuck in my throat, blocked by a lump of dread that tasted like metal. My mind was spinning, and concentration had escaped my every thought. All I wanted was to ask God to tell me it wasn't true—to rewind the morning, to give me a different road to drive down.

Steph grabbed the keys and jumped in the driver's seat. She was quiet. Steph's silence has different textures. There is the peaceful silence of a Sunday afternoon on the porch, and there is the heavy, loaded silence of a soldier waiting for the first shot to be fired. This was the latter. She was preparing for war.

She reached over and placed her hand on my arm. She did not squeeze; she just rested it there. An anchor in the storm.

"Whatever it is," she said, her voice steady, betraying none of the fear I knew she felt, "we will handle it."

"I know," I said.

In reality though, I didn't.

I had spent the last six months rebuilding my life after the first cancer scare. I had done the surgery in February—the partial nephrectomy that took part of my kidney. I had done the recovery, sleeping upright in a chair for weeks. I had walked the halls of the hospital, shuffling in non-slip socks, and rung the bell proclaiming I was cancer free in my mind, if not in reality. I thought the book was closed. I thought I was in the epilogue of the cancer story, the part where the hero walks into the sunset, scarred but alive.

I had even returned to work, traveling again, feeling the old energy return. I felt invincible. I thought I had eaten my turnip greens—I had swallowed the bitter pill of Stage 2, and now I was owed the dessert of a long, healthy life.

As we pulled into the parking lot of the medical center, a cold dread settled in my gut. It felt heavy, familiar, and suffocating. It felt like a door slamming shut.

We walked into the building. The doors slid open with a whoosh. The smell hit me first—that specific, sterile mix of antiseptic, stale coffee, and nervous sweat that permeates every doctor's office in America. It is the scent of vulnerability.

The receptionist looked up. Usually, there is paperwork. Usually, there is a wait. Usually, you sit in the chairs, thumbing through a three-year-old magazine, watching the clock.

"Mr. Herrin," she said. She did not ask for my insurance card. She did not tell me to have a seat.

She simply nodded and then a nurse opened the door to the hallway.

"Right this way."

No waiting room. That was the final nail. If they do not make you wait, it is because the news cannot wait.

We walked down the long hallway. My footsteps sounded too loud on the linoleum. *Click. Click. Click.* I felt like a dead man walking. I looked at the photos on the wall—generic landscapes, calming beaches, scenes of tranquility meant to lower your blood pressure. They had the opposite effect. They felt fake. They felt like lies.

We entered the exam room. I sat on the crinkly paper of the exam table, then stood up immediately. I could not sit. The energy in my legs was frantic, a fight-or-flight response with nowhere to go. I paced the small room. Three steps one way. Turn. Three steps back.

Steph sat in the guest chair, right beside me, her hands folded in her lap. She was praying. I knew she was praying because her breathing had shifted into a slow, rhythmic pattern. She was building the spiritual walls that would hold us up when the physical ones came crashing down.

The doctor walked in. He was a good man. A kind man. We had built a relationship over the years. He usually walked in with a smile, a handshake, a joke about the Georgia heat or a football game.

Today, he walked in holding a folder against his chest like a shield. He did not smile. He did not shake my hand. He looked at me with his eyes filled with profound, professional sorrow. He looked tired.

He sat down on the rolling stool and sighed, a heavy exhale that took all the air out of the room.

"Jerry," he said. "Please sit down."

I sat. The paper crinkled beneath me, a sound that seemed deafening in the quiet.

The room was too still for the words he was about to say. The fluorescent lights hummed overhead, casting everything in a sterile, unreal glow. I stared at the diploma on the wall behind his head, trying to focus on the gold foil seal, trying to focus on anything but the folder in his hands.

He cleared his throat.

"I'm sorry, Jerry," he said softly. "The scans show that the cancer is back."

I stopped breathing. My heart stuttered.

"And," he continued, his voice dropping an octave, "it has metastasized. It is in your lungs. There are multiple nodules. It's Stage 4."

For a moment, the world stopped.

The rush of blood in my ears drowned out the hum of the lights. Steph's grip on my hand tightened until it hurt, her fingernails digging into my skin. I wanted to say something, anything, but the words caught in my throat.

Stage 4.

That was not a diagnosis. It was a sentence.

Stage 1 is a scare. Stage 2 is a battle. Stage 3 is a war. But Stage 4? Stage 4 is where hope goes to die. At least, that's what it felt like. It felt like an expiration date stamped on my forehead.

I looked at him in disbelief. "My lungs?" I whispered.

He nodded. "Yes. It moved fast. Faster than we expected."

I had spent my life fighting for control, for certainty, for the next rung on the ladder. I was a fixer. I was a manager. I was the guy you called when things went wrong. But in that moment, sitting in that cold room, stripped of my titles and my illusions, all I could do was breathe and try not to fall apart.

"What now?" Steph asked. Her voice was strong, stronger than mine.

"We treat it," he said. "But we can't cure it. We treat for time."

Time...

Suddenly, time was not something I measured in quarters or fiscal years. It was measured in breaths. It was measured in Christmases. It was measured in moments I might miss.

That was the day my story split into two parts: Before and After.

Before, cancer was something that happened to other people. It was a sad commercial on TV with sad music. It was a prayer request at church for someone you barely knew. It was a ribbon on a bumper sticker.

After, it was the air I breathed. It was the first thought when I woke up and the last thought before I slept.

I did not know it then, but that diagnosis would become the foundation of my faith. It would burn down the house of ego I had built over forty years and force me to live in the shelter of God's grace. It would teach me that I am not the author of my story, only the main character.

This is the story of After.

CHAPTER 1

Roots & Rules

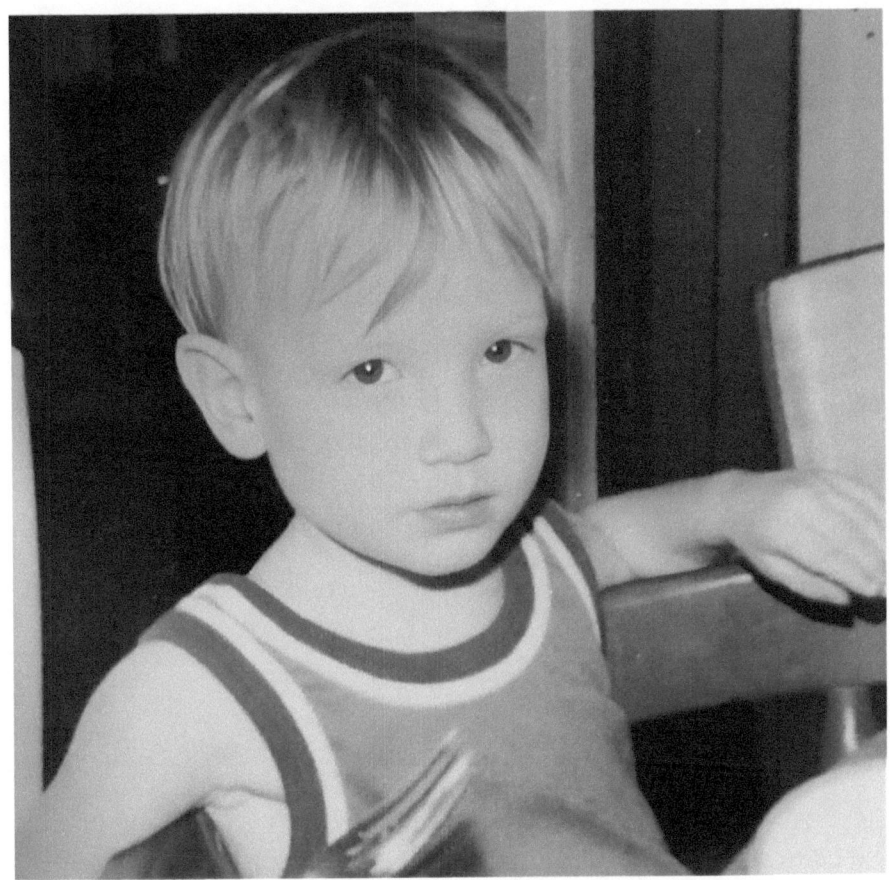

I was sixteen years old the first time I punched a clock.

The year was 1991. The place was Giant Foods in Warner Robins, Georgia.

If you closed your eyes and walked inside, you would know exactly where you were by the smell alone. It was a distinct, heavy mixture of brown paper bags, industrial lemon floor wax, and produce misting on a timer. It was not glamorous. The floors were hard, the lighting was harsh, and the air conditioning was always set just a few degrees too cold. But to me, it smelled like opportunity. It smelled like independence.

At sixteen, I did not want a handout. I wanted honest work. I wanted my own money in my pocket.

The store manager was a man named Bill. Bill was a legend in his own small way—a thick-handed man with a permanent squint etched into his face from years spent beneath those buzzing fluorescent lights. He was not big on speeches. He did not waste words. When he spoke, the air in the room seemed to get heavier, and you paid attention.

I still remember the first time I approached him. I stood in the frozen food aisle, shivering slightly in my T-shirt, holding a paper job application that I had filled out in my neatest handwriting. I waited for him to finish checking inventory on frozen peas.

Finally, he turned. He looked at me, then at the paper, then back at me.

"I'll look it over," he grunted.

He took the paper and walked away.

A week had passed. I heard nothing. I went back. I found him by the dairy section. "Just checking on my application, sir." He nodded, not breaking his stride. "I'm still looking."

Another week passed. I filled out a second application, just in case the first one had vanished into the ether of the back office. I went back a third time.

This time, I found him in the front office. I stood in the doorway, refusing to leave.

Finally, Bill stopped what he was doing. He put his pen down on the desk with a definitive *click*. He looked me over from head to toe, studying me like I was a bruised apple he was deciding whether to toss or keep.

"You're persistent, aren't you?" he said.

I stood up straighter, trying to look like a man instead of a high school kid with a bad haircut. "I'm a hard worker, sir. I just need an opportunity to prove it."

He paused long enough for my heart to hammer a rhythm against my ribs. I held his gaze. My dad had taught me that—never look down when you are asking a man for something.

Finally, Bill nodded. "Alright. I'll give you ninety days."

To a sixteen-year-old kid, it was like I had won the lottery. Ninety days. It was a trial, a test, a challenge. And I loved the challenge.

Bill ran that store with military precision. He had spent his early years selling cars before marrying into the grocery business, and he believed in structure. He did not believe in "good enough." He believed in "right."

My uniform was non-negotiable: a white dress shirt and a black tie. And not just any shirt—it had to be hand-starched stiff enough to stand on its own. My mom taught me how to use spray starch and the iron until the creases were sharp enough to cut paper. Hair trimmed clean, off the ears. No facial hair. No excuses.

The job was simple on paper: smile, bag the groceries, and treat every customer like they were the most important person in the world.

But I realized quickly that bagging groceries was not just about putting food in sacks. It was architecture. You had to build a foundation with the cans and boxes, create structure with the jars, and lay the fragile items—the bread, the eggs, the chips—on top like a roof. Do it wrong, and you crushed the bread. Crush the bread, and you lost the customer.

I did not know it then, but that grocery store aisle was where I first learned to sell.

The real currency was not the minimum wage; it was the tips. We carried groceries out to the cars for the customers. That walk from the automatic doors to the trunk of a Buick was my sales floor. The more care you gave, the more you earned.

You learned to read people. You learned that Mrs. Johnson wanted to talk about her grandkids, so you asked about them. You learned that Mr. Smith was in a hurry, so you moved fast and kept your mouth shut.

When a regular customer stepped into line—the kind known for tipping a dollar if you did not smash their bread—you found a little extra speed in your stride. You hustled to open a new register. It was not greed, though. It was hustle. It was the immediate feedback loop of service and reward.

Bill taught us to take pride in the small things. He would walk the aisles, spot a stray receipt on the floor from twenty feet away, and point at it.

"Leave things better than you found them," he would say. "Do your work so well that no one has to come behind you to fix it."

I would leave work smelling like detergent and produce, my shoes squeaking from mopped floors, my feet aching, but I walked out tall.

That job taught me that service, no matter how small, is a sort of ministry. Holding a door, offering a smile, or listening to a lonely customer's story—it was good work if done with the right heart.

If the grocery store was my first classroom, my home was the sanctuary where those lessons were born.

We were not rich by any measure. We were modestly middle class, coming from a small town and a small family. But we were steady. Steady in faith, steady in love, and steady in the kind of discipline that kept you honest.

My dad believed in two things: God and hard work. He had grown up in a part of Georgia most folks drove through without noticing—a stretch of two-lane roads and pine trees that hummed in the heat. For him, life was not about finding yourself; it was about creating yourself. Joining the military was his way out, his shot at something bigger.

Mom met him not long after, in a small church in the middle of nowhere. She came from almost nothing but possessed a heart that could make something out of anything. They married only two weeks after meeting.

Two weeks.

I realize it was not recklessness; it was faith. They believed love was a decision first and a feeling second. They made a covenant, and they spent the rest of their lives honoring it. That decision became the foundation of our lives.

Our house was run with a rhythm of structure, respect, and purpose. When Dad came through the door in uniform, the atmosphere shifted. He was not harsh, just precise. Everything had a place. Beds were made tight enough to bounce a quarter off the sheets. Shoes were lined by the door like soldiers waiting for inspection.

If Dad was the order, Mom was the warmth. She was a steady mix of Southern grace and quiet determination. She believed in good manners, clean clothes, and keeping your word. She did not need to raise her voice to get her point across; she had the "Mom Look." One glance could stop me in my tracks faster than any punishment.

Growing up, we knew two things: chores and table manners.

Dinner was sacred. Most nights, Mom cooked and we ate together. There were no TVs on. No distractions. Just us. Sometimes the meal was something Dad had caught or harvested like venison or fish. Other times, it was his favorite: potato soup and crackling cornbread.

Whatever was on the plate, you finished it. If you complained, you were reminded about the children in other countries who would give anything for a meal as fine as the one Mom had prepared.

This leads me to the title of this book. To understand who I am, you must understand the sheer will of my mother when it came to vegetables. Specifically, turnip greens.

There was a specific Tuesday night that I still remember like a war movie. The enemy? A steaming dark-green pile of boiled leaves sitting in the center of my plate.

Turnip greens have a distinct smell. It is earthy, heavy, and pungent. To a ten-year-old boy who just wanted to go outside and ride his bike, that smell was the scent of captivity.

The rule in our house was simple: You eat what is served, and you do not leave the table until the plate is clean.

There was a specific Tuesday night that I **still remember** like a war movie.

The enemy? A steaming dark-green pile of boiled leaves sitting in the center of my plate.

By then, I had already learned the rules of the table.

That night, I sat there, staring at the greens. They looked like wet seaweed. I tried every trick in the book. The "hide it under the cornbread" maneuver. "Washing" them down with sweet tea and even "the slow-play," hoping that they'd get tired and let me off easy or even send me to bed.

They did not get tired.

Mom washed the dishes. Dad watched TV or tinkered. I sat there staring at the greens as they went from hot to lukewarm to cold.

"They're not going anywhere, Jerry," Dad said, not even looking up from the show he was watching.

"They taste like dirt," I argued, my voice trembling.

"That's the minerals," Mom chimed in, wiping down the counter. "It's good for your muscles. Eat."

It became a standoff. Me vs. The Greens.

I eventually ate them, one bitter forkful at a time, washing them down with tears and sweet tea. I was miserable. I felt like I was being punished.

But looking back, I realize what was happening at that table. My parents were not trying to torture me; they were trying to fortify me. They knew that the world was going to be hard. They knew I would need iron in my blood to survive it. They loved me enough to make me do the thing I hated because they knew it was the thing I needed.

That memory became my anchor forty years later. When the doctor handed me the diagnosis—the ultimate bowl of bitter greens—I wanted to push the plate away. I wanted to leave the table.

But I heard my father's voice, gentle but firm: *This is not going anywhere, Jerry. Eat. It will make you strong.*

Two things went into those meals: Time and love. Both deserved gratitude.

Those dinners were leadership seminars disguised as supper. We learned respect. You waited your turn to speak. No elbows on the table. No interrupting adults. And when you spoke, you looked people in the eye.

Dad used to say, "A man's word is his bond."

Ours was a cash-only household. No checking accounts. No credit cards. If you could not pay for it today, you did not need it today. It felt old-fashioned then, but that discipline carved out a lifelong respect for living within my means. When the world screams for more status and more things, I remember my parents counting bills at the kitchen table, never once complaining about what we lacked.

I remember asking my mom once, "Are we poor?"

She smiled and gave me the same answer she always did. **"We may be poor in money, Jerry, but we're rich in love."**

It sounded like a cliché to a kid who just wanted the cool sneakers his friends had. But she was right. We were rich in things that could not be bought.

Being the only boy with two older sisters taught me diplomacy early on. They were strong-willed, quick-witted, and fiercely protective. They did not tolerate laziness, and if I tried to skip a chore, they caught me. But Lord help anyone outside the house who tried to mess with their little brother. They taught me to respect women, to listen before speaking, and to value different perspectives.

But for all the structure and love, I was not a model student.

By the time I hit my junior and senior years of high school, I had dug myself into a deep academic hole. I liked the social aspect of school, but the books did not hold my interest. My grades slipped. Then they plummeted. By the time reality set in, my GPA was too low to graduate on time with my class. I had to pivot from college prep to vocational studies to make the math work, but even that would prove challenging.

The easy route would have been to quit, or to get a GED, but my parents would not hear of it.

"If you start quitting now," Dad said, standing in the living room, his arms crossed, "you'll quit for the rest of your life."

So, the decision was made and I went to night school.

While my friends were going to movies or cruising town, I sat under flickering lights in classrooms that smelled of chalk dust and stale coffee. It was humbling. The popular kids or the high achievers did not surround me; around me were people who, like me, had stumbled but refused to stay down. There were single moms, guys working two jobs, people fighting for a second chance.

I learned something in those nights that no textbook ever taught me: discipline is not built through success; it is forged in struggle.

When I finally walked across that graduation stage, I did not walk as a scholar. I walked as a survivor. I held that diploma tighter than any of the valedictorians held theirs, because I knew the price I had paid for it.

I tried college for one semester to make my parents proud. But sitting in those lecture halls, watching students furiously take notes on theory, I felt suffocated. I did not know what I wanted to become, but I knew it was not going to be found in a textbook.

I needed to work. I needed to build something with my own hands. I needed to be in the arena, not watching from the stands.

That need led me to the glass doors of a local Toyota dealership.

My brother-in-law, Ray, sold cars in North Carolina. He painted a picture of a world that was fast-paced, competitive, and full of opportunity—a place where hustle could outwork education. It was the first time I saw that success might be something you could hunt down rather than inherit.

When I told my parents I was leaving college to sell cars, the silence in the kitchen was heavy.

Mom laughed first. "Sell cars? Jerry, you can barely talk to a girl without blushing. How are you going to sell a car to a stranger?"

Dad was less subtle. He raised an eyebrow, looking at me like I had just announced I was joining the circus.

"You're going to make a mistake," he said flatly. "You'll never make it in car sales. You need a real job, or you need to join the military."

His doubt stung. It cut deep. But it also lit a fire in my belly that has not gone out to this day.

I did not see myself in the military. I did not see myself in the classroom. But standing on the edge of the dealership lot, looking at the rows of shining metal and realizing that my paycheck depended entirely on my own effort?

That, I could see.

I had no idea what I was doing. I had no degree, no experience, and no backup plan. But I had the roots my parents had given me. I knew how to say "yes, sir," I knew how to look a man in the eye, and thanks to Bill, I knew how to starch a shirt.

I was nineteen years old. I was terrified. I was ready to work.

CHAPTER 2

The Car Business & the "Old Dog"
Part 1: The Shark Tank

The day I walked into the Toyota dealership for the first time, I was not just walking into a job; I was stepping into a different universe.

It was 1994. I was nineteen years old. I had no college degree, no connections, and a suit that did not fit. It hung off my shoulders a little too loosely, the fabric cheap and stiff, making me look exactly like what I was: a kid wearing his dad's clothes, trying to play a man's game.

If the grocery store had been a world of order, politeness, and starch, the car business was a jungle. The moment the automatic glass doors slid open, the atmosphere hit me. It was not a smell you could wash off easily. It was a cocktail of new rubber from the tires on the showroom floor, stale coffee burning on a burner in the breakroom, industrial floor cleaner, and high-octane ambition.

It was a place where silence made people nervous. Phones were ringing constantly—a shrill, mechanical chorus. The intercom buzzed every thirty seconds, paging sales reps to the tower, paging service advisors to the lane, paging customers to the finance box.

I walked toward the sales desk, trying to adopt a stride that looked confident, but inside, my stomach was doing backflips. Once I crossed that threshold, I was on my own.

At the center of the showroom sat the "Tower." In the car business, the Tower is the raised desk where the sales managers sit. It is designed to be intimidating. It sits higher than the rest of the floor, giving the managers a panoramic view of the lot, the showroom, and the salespeople. It is the judge's bench, the throne room, and the principal's office all rolled into one.

A manager with a thick New Jersey accent and a face that looked like it had been chiseled out of granite looked up from a stack of deal jackets. He did not offer a hand. He did not smile. He just looked me up and down, his eyes scanning me like I was a trade-in vehicle with high mileage and a cracked windshield. He was assessing my value, and by the look on his face, the appraisal was not coming in high.

"How you doing, Brah?" he asked. He was chewing on something—gum, a pen cap, or a toothpick. He did not stop chewing to talk.

"I'm good, sir," I said, my voice sounding thinner than I wanted it to. "First day."

He smirked. It was not a friendly smile; it was the kind of grin that says he knows the punchline to a joke you have not heard yet. He turned to the guy sitting next to him, pointing a gold pen in my direction.

"I'll give him two weeks."

I blinked, confused. I looked from him to his partner. "Two weeks to sell a car?" I asked, hopefully.

He laughed, a sharp, barking sound that echoed off the tile floor. "No, kid. Two weeks before you quit or get fired."

Those words hit me like a physical slap. Combined with the look on my father's face when I told him I was leaving college to sell cars—that look of disappointed resignation—they formed a heavy, cold knot in my stomach.

Doubt. Discouragement. Low expectations.

It was the same sinking sensation I had felt in high school when I looked at my failing grades. It was the voice that whispered, *You do not belong here. You are not cut out for the real world.*

The manager turned back to his paperwork, dismissing me as if I were already gone. To him, I was just a ghost passing through. Another "green pea" who would burn out, blow out, and disappear before the month was over.

But as I stood there, watching the top of his head, feeling the heat rise in my cheeks, that knot in my stomach tightened into something else. It hardened.

That become my fuel.

I decided right then and there, standing on that polished showroom floor: *I am not going to quit in two weeks. I am not going to quit in two years. I am going to prove every single one of them wrong.*

🙶🙶🙶

The first few months were a blur of long hours, trial by fire, and pure, unadulterated exhaustion.

Selling cars was not like selling groceries.

In a grocery store, people come to you because they need food. They are typically happy to see you. They need milk, bread, and eggs. You provide a service, they say thank you, and they leave. It is transactional, but it is friendly.

In a dealership, people come to you with their guard up. They walk onto the lot assuming you are a liar. They assume you are out to cheat them, rob them, and take advantage of them. Every customer was a battle. Every handshake was a test of wills.

I had some success early on, mostly because I did not know enough to be scared. I ran on pure energy. If a customer wanted to see a car at the back of the lot in the pouring Georgia rain, I did not walk—I sprinted to get the keys. I did not care about getting my cheap suit wet.

If someone stayed until 10 p.m. debating a fifty-dollar difference in monthly payments, I stayed until 10:01. I was the first one through the doors in the morning, and I was the last one to leave, watching the lot lights flicker off.

But raw effort only takes you so far. The more I learned about selling, the more I stumbled.

I became desperate to sell. And in sales, desperation is like cheap cologne—if you wear too much of it, people can smell it from a mile away, and it drives them off. It makes them gag.

I was rushing the process. I was talking too fast, trying to fill every silence with facts and figures, trying too hard to be liked. I took every "no" personally. When a customer walked out, it felt like a rejection of *me*, not the car. It felt like confirmation of what my dad had said, of what the manager had bet on.

I started to feel invisible. And making matters worse were the "Old Dogs."

To understand the pressure I was under, you must understand the environment of the car business in the mid-nineties. It was not the corporate, sanitized, HR-compliant environment it is today. It was the Wild West.

The "Old Dogs," the veteran salespeople, were a breed of their own. They were the lions of the showroom, and they looked at me like a gazelle with a limp.

They stood in clusters by the front door, smoking cigarettes, watching the lot like hawks. They wore suits that had seen better days, often shiny at the elbows, and carried heavy gold lighters that *clinked* loudly when they closed them. Their skin was leathery from years of standing on asphalt in the southern sun.

They guarded their trade secrets like gold. They did not want to help the new guy; they wanted to starve him out so there was more commission for them.

They could tell you a customer's credit score just by looking at the shoes they wore or the trade-in they drove.

"Look at that," one would whisper, exhaling a cloud of smoke. "Bald tires, McDonald's bags in the back seat. That is a 450 credit score walking. Don't waste your time."

And they were usually right.

They had a language all their own, a code that I could not crack. A "lay-down" was an easy sale—someone who paid sticker price without a fight. A "bogue" was a customer with bad credit who could not buy a bicycle, let alone a Camry. A "green pea" was a new guy like me.

I watched them. I studied them. I saw how they could switch their personalities in a split second—charming one moment with a customer, asking about their grandkids, laughing at jokes that were not funny. Then, the moment they walked into the sales office, the mask dropped. They became ruthless, fighting the managers for every dime of commission, cursing the inventory, manipulating the system. It was an art performance.

But I also saw the cost.

I saw the guys who slept in their cars in the back lot because they had been kicked out of their houses by wives who could not take the hours anymore. I saw the guys who popped antacids like candy, their faces red with high blood pressure. I saw the guys who had heart attacks at forty-five because their bodies were running on stress and caffeine. I saw the guys who made six figures a year but had no one to share it with because they had missed every birthday, anniversary, and ball game for the last decade.

It was a seductive world because the cash was immediate. You could sell a car at 10 a.m. and have a "spiff" (a cash bonus) in your pocket by noon. A hundred dollars. Two hundred dollars. Just for selling a unit. It made you feel rich, even if you were broke. It taught me to hustle, yes. But it also taught me that if you are not careful, you can sell your soul for a commission check.

I realized early on that I had a choice to make. Was I going to become one of the "Old Dogs," hardened, cynical, and alone? Or could I survive in this jungle without becoming an animal?

The schedule was brutal. We worked "bell-to-bell" shifts. That meant you were there when the bell rang to open the store, and you were there when the bell rang to close it. Twelve, fourteen hours a day. You ate vending machine crackers for lunch because you were afraid if you left the lot to get a sandwich, you would miss an "up"—a customer walking on the lot.

"You leave the lot, you lose the lot," the veterans would say.

So, I stayed. I starved. I drank coffee until my hands shook.

By month three, the adrenaline was wearing off. My numbers were slipping. I was barely selling eight cars a month—just enough to keep my job, but not enough to make a living. The draw (the minimum wage advance they pay you against your future commissions) was eating up my paychecks. I was working seventy hours a week and making less than I did bagging groceries.

The doubt was creeping in. The "two weeks" comment echoed in my head every night as I drove home in the dark. *Maybe they were right*, I thought. *I do not have the killer instinct.*

I was tired. I was frustrated. And I was scared that my dad was right—that I had made a terrible mistake.

That is when I met Greg.

❦❦❦

As you often find in the car business, change is the only thing consistent. It often felt like ownership would bring in a new management team every six to twelve months to replace the last, unhappy with whatever the results may be and assuming there is something better.

It would not be the first time I had experienced change, but it would be the most impactful to date.

Greg was the General Sales Manager. If the sales managers on the tower were the judges, Greg was the Supreme Court.

To a nineteen-year-old kid, he was terrifying. He was a commanding figure, broad-shouldered with a booming voice and a reputation that made the whole showroom straighten up when he walked through the glass doors. He did not suffer fools, and he did not tolerate laziness. He could strip the paint off the walls with his voice if he caught you slacking off.

For me, Greg represented judgment day. I avoided him at all costs. I tried to fly under the radar, hoping he would not notice the struggling kid in the corner.

One Tuesday afternoon, I was working with a couple on the new car lot. It was a hot day, the kind where the heat radiates off the asphalt and melts the rubber soles of your shoes. The couple was looking at a Corolla. They were nice, but they were firm.

"We're just looking," the husband said. "We're not buying today."

I tried my lines. I tried to overcome the objection. But I was tired. I was beaten down. And honestly, I did not want to drag them inside and have a manager grind on them for an hour. I liked them. I did not want to subject them to the "process."

The dealership rule was simple, written in stone: If you let a customer leave without speaking to a manager (a "turnover" or T.O.), you might as well leave with them. It was the cardinal sin of the car business. You never, ever let a customer walk without a second face.

But I was frustrated. So, when they walked toward their car, I let them go.

"Thanks for coming in," I said. "Here's my card."

I did not wave a manager over. I did not try to stop them. I watched them get into their Ford and drive away.

I looked around. The coast seemed clear. No managers on the lot. I exhaled, feeling a mix of relief and guilt. I had spared them, but I had broken the code.

I walked back toward the showroom, wiping sweat from my forehead, hoping to sneak back to my desk unnoticed.

Then, the PA system crackled to life. It was a sound that made every salesperson freeze.

"Jerry Herrin. Come to Greg's office immediately."

The blood drained from my face. My stomach twisted into knots so tight I thought I might throw up. I knew it was over. He had seen me. He had been watching from the window.

I was getting fired.

I walked the long hallway to his office like a man walking to the gallows. Every step felt heavy. I passed the other salespeople, and they would not look at me. They knew. When you get called to the principal's office like that, you do not come back.

I reached his door. It was open.

Greg was sitting behind his desk. He was not looking at paperwork. He was not on the phone. He was looking straight at the empty chair in front of him. His face was red.

I stepped inside. "You wanted to see me, sir?"

He did not yell. That would have been easier. If he had yelled, I could have gotten defensive. Instead, he just stared at me. The silence stretched out for what felt like an hour. The air conditioner hummed in the corner, the only sound in the room.

"Sit down," he said. His voice was low, dangerous.

I sat. I waited for the hammer to fall. I waited for him to tell me to pack my box.

He leaned forward, placing his elbows on the desk. "You know the rules, Jerry."

"Yes, sir."

"You let them walk."

"Yes, sir."

"Why?"

I wanted to lie. I wanted to say they had an emergency, or that they promised to come back. But looking at Greg, I knew lying would be fatal.

"I...I did not think they were buyers," I stammered. "I didn't want to waste your time."

He stared at me for another long moment. Then he did something I did not expect. He sighed. He shifted in his chair, and the anger in his face softened just a fraction. It was replaced by something that looked like…curiosity.

"Jerry," he said, "how long have you been here?"

"A little over a year, sir."

"And how many cars did you sell last month?"

"Six."

He nodded. "Six cars. You're starving."

"Yes, sir."

He pointed a finger at me. "I've been watching you. You run around this lot like your hair is on fire. You work harder than most of the guys out there. You know the product better than guys who have been here for five years."

I looked up, surprised. He had noticed.

"But," he continued, his voice firming up, "you talk too much. You rush the process. You're trying so hard to be liked that you're forgetting to lead the customer."

He leaned back in his chair. "You're chasing approval, Jerry. Stop chasing approval. Start building confidence."

He did not fire me.

"I'm not going to fire you today," he said. "Because I see something in you. You have potential. You don't even see it yet, but I do."

Tears pricked the corners of my eyes. It was the first time since I started that anyone told me I had potential.

"But we're going to fix this," he said. "From now on, you don't talk until the customer talks. You listen. You slow down. You stop acting like a desperate kid and start acting like a professional."

That conversation changed the trajectory of my life. Greg became the first real mentor I had ever had in the business world. He saw the insecurity masking itself as hustle, and he decided to help me fix it.

He started calling me "Howard Hughes."

At first, I did not get it. Howard Hughes was eccentric, brilliant, and eventually a recluse who stored his urine in jars. Was he making fun of me?

"Think about it," Greg said one afternoon when I asked him about it. "Hughes was obsessive. He saw details no one else saw. He was a perfectionist. You have that same intensity, Jerry. You obsess over the details of the car. If you can channel that intensity into understanding people instead of just impressing them, you'll be dangerous."

He taught me the art of slowing down.

"Selling isn't about talking," he told me. "It's about listening long enough to understand what someone cares about, then showing them why it relates. People don't buy cars because they understand the engine; they buy cars because they feel understood."

That one sentence shifted everything.

I stopped trying to "sell" a car and started trying to listen and solve the problem. I began watching body language. I listened to the hesitation in a customer's voice when they talked about monthly payments. I stopped treating them like targets and started treating them like people who feared making a bad decision.

As I learned to slow down, I also began to realize another passion: the product itself.

Part 2: The Fire and the Walkaround

My obsession with details, which Greg had noticed, began to pay off in ways I had not expected. I developed a passion for the product itself, specifically Toyota.

To understand this, you must understand where I came from. In the South, trucks are not just vehicles; they are members of the family. My first vehicle had been a 1984 Toyota pickup. It was dependable, tough, and simple. It started every time I turned the key. That truck represented freedom.

But my passion was not just about the metal; it was ignited by a man named Bill. A man we referred to as "Rev," short for Reverend.

Bill worked for the manufacturer. He was a product trainer for Toyota. When new models were released, it was Bill's job to travel across the Southeast, stand in front of hundreds of eager salespeople in large hotel ballrooms, racetracks, or runways, and help us see the value in what we were selling.

Bill did not just teach; he performed. He was a force of nature. He had fire, enthusiasm, and a passion that was contagious. He would be up on stage, under the hot lights, sweating bullets as he did a walkaround on a new Camry or 4Runner. He did not just point at the engine; he evangelized it. He made you feel like you were not just selling a car; you were selling the greatest machine ever built.

Watching Bill was one of my first true inspirations as a young professional. I sat in the audience, mesmerized, thinking, *I want to have that*. I wanted to lead with that same passion, energy, and enthusiasm because I saw how it lit up the room. I saw that when people are excited and enthusiastic about the product, they inevitably get better results.

I realized then that success is not about technique. It is about belief. If you are not passionate about the product you are selling or the place where you work, you will never reach your full potential. Customers can smell apathy a mile away. But they can also feel belief. Belief is magnetic.

I started to see that leadership—whether leading a customer to a sale or leading a team to a goal—is like a recipe. It is not just one thing. You must have the passion for what you are doing. You must care about the success of others more than your own. You must believe in those around you and help them believe in themselves when they do not. And you must empower them so they feel their contributions matter.

But the most important part of the recipe is the execution: ensuring that all those ingredients balance with your true authentic self. Bill was authentic. He was not faking the sweat. He loved those cars.

I wanted to be the Bill of my dealership.

That ambition led to my first significant professional win.

The dealership announced a local "Walkaround Competition." For those outside the industry, a walkaround is exactly what it sounds like—you walk around the car with the customer, popping the hood, opening the doors, pointing out features, and explaining benefits.

Most salespeople treated the walkaround like a chore. They wanted to skip it and get to the test drive. But I channeled Bill. I decided I was not just going to present the car; I was going to put on a show.

I poured everything into preparation. I studied every weld, every safety feature, every crumple zone. I memorized the cargo capacity down to the cubic inch. I learned why the engine mounts were placed where they were.

When the day of the competition arrived, the vehicle selected for the presentation was a 1995 Toyota Corolla Station Wagon.

You must laugh at that now. It was not a Supra. It was not a Land Cruiser. It was a beige station wagon—a grocery-getter. Most of the "Old Dogs" rolled their eyes. How were you supposed to make a station wagon exciting?

But I remembered Bill. I remembered that passion is not about the object; it is about the story you tell about the object.

I stood in front of the judges—managers from the dealership and a representative from Southeast Toyota. In the back of the room, the veteran salespeople stood with their arms crossed, leaning against the wall, smirking. They expected me to choke.

I took a deep breath. I remembered Greg's advice: *Stop chasing approval. Start building confidence.* And I remembered Bill's energy.

I walked to the front of the vehicle. "This isn't just a bumper," I said, tapping the composite material with conviction. "This is a five-mile-per-hour impact absorber. That means when someone backs into you at the grocery store, it bounces back instead of cracking, saving you a five-hundred-dollar deductible."

I moved to the side. I opened the rear door. "Look at this door beam. It is steel. It is reinforced. If you have a child sitting in this seat, this beam is the shield that keeps them safe."

I was not selling a car anymore; I was selling peace of mind. I was selling safety for a family. I was selling reliability. I was sweating, just like Bill, but I felt electric.

I won.

They handed me a trophy and a cash prize. To some, it might have been a small contest in a small town, but to me, it was validation. It proved that if you respect the product, respect the process, and bring your authentic passion to the table, the results follow.

Part 3: The Hustle

The car business has a wicked way of keeping you humble. Just as I was finding my footing, confident in my new skills from the Walkaround victory, the ground shifted beneath me.

Greg left to work for the manufacturer. Then the rumor mill started churning. *The store is for sale.*

In the car business, a sale is usually bad news for the employees. It means a purge is coming. And sure enough, the dealership was sold.

Overnight, the culture changed. A new ownership group came in from out of state. They brought their own management team, their own rules, and their own agenda. The family atmosphere evaporated, replaced by a cold, corporate factory mentality.

The new managers did not know about my Walkaround trophy. They did not know about my late nights or my dedication. They looked at the sales board, looked at my year-to-date numbers, and shrugged.

"What have you done for me today?" was the new motto.

My numbers slipped. My income dropped. The confidence Greg and Bill had helped me build started to crack. The "Old Dogs" were grumbling, talking about quitting, talking about the "good old days." The toxicity in the showroom was palpable.

But this time, instead of panicking, I remembered the lesson of the grocery store: *Hustle creates opportunity.*

I looked around for an edge. I needed something that would make me indispensable to the new regime.

At the time, short-term leasing was exploding in the auto industry. It was a new way of buying—driving a new car every two or three years for a lower payment. But the contracts were complex. The math was confusing. Residual values, money factors, acquisition fees, capitalized cost reductions—it was a foreign language.

Most of the old-school salespeople hated it. They refused to learn it.

"It's a fad," they grumbled, lighting another cigarette. "It's a scam. Just sell 'em the car, Jerry. Don't confuse 'em with that lease garbage."

I realized that their refusal was my opportunity.

I decided to become the expert they refused to be.

I took the lease manuals home. I studied them at the kitchen table until my eyes blurred. I learned the math backward and forward. I learned how to explain the value to a customer in plain English—how they could drive more car for less money, how they could avoid negative equity, how they could stay under warranty forever.

Soon, I was not just selling my own deals, I was helping the veterans sell theirs.

It started slowly. One of the Old Dogs, a guy named Cedric who had been around for years, waved me over to his desk one busy Saturday. He had a young couple who wanted a Camry but could not afford the payments on a traditional loan.

"Hey, Jerry," Cedric called, "come run those lease numbers for these folks."

I sat down. I walked the couple through the lease. I drew a diagram on a piece of paper, showing them the difference between buying the whole car and just paying for the part they used. I saw the lightbulb go on in their eyes.

"We'll take it," the husband said.

Cedric looked at me, stunned. He had been trying to close them for two hours. I closed them in ten minutes.

If the deal closed, I earned a split of the commission. It was not a lot of money, but it bought me something more valuable than cash: respect.

I made myself indispensable.

That season of hustling for lease deals taught me something surprising: I did not just like selling; I liked teaching too.

There is a specific look a customer gives you when the math finally clicks—when the confusion vanishes and is replaced by relief. For months, I had been chasing that look. But soon, I started seeing it on the faces of the other salespeople, too.

When I helped the veterans structure their deals, I was not just doing the math for them; I was explaining the *why* behind it. I realized that knowledge was not just power, it was currency. And unlike money, you did not lose it when you gave it away. When I shared what I knew, the whole floor got better.

The new ownership noticed. They saw that the kid who walked fast and obsessed over details was also the guy everyone turned to when a deal was stuck.

They decided to invest in that spark. They sent me to a week-long "Train the Trainer" certification course.

At the time, I thought it was just another corporate seminar. I expected bad coffee, a three-ring binder, and a lot of boredom. I packed my bag, expecting a week off from the grind.

I was wrong. It was a masterclass in communication.

For three days, I was drilled not on *what* to say, but *how* to say it. I learned that teaching is not about dumping information; it is about building a bridge. You must meet people who are skeptical, tired, or confused—and walk them across the bridge to understanding.

We role-played until my brain hurt. I stood at the front of the room, sweating, trying to explain complex sales concepts while the instructor critiqued my body language, my tone, and my pacing.

"You're moving too fast, Jerry," the instructor would say, cutting me off. "You lost the room. Slow down. Look them in the eye. Make sure they're with you."

Slow down.

It was the same lesson Greg had taught me but now it was applied to leadership. It was not about selling a car anymore; it was about selling an idea. It was about influence.

I came back from that week with a new toolkit. I was not just a guy who knew how to close a deal; I was a guy who could replicate that success in others.

That course became the foundation of my leadership style. Years later, when I was leading hundreds of people, I would look back on that week as the turning point. It moved me from being a "Doer" to being a "Developer."

I realized that a leader's legacy is not built on their own performance; it is built on their ability to transfer their passion to the person standing next to them, just like Bill did for me.

And I was ready to transfer everything I had.

CHAPTER 3

The Passover

Part 1: The Bitter Taste of Entitlement

To this point, I was learning how to survive the jungle. My next lesson would be about what happens when you start to believe you own it.

It started with a victory that felt like the finish line, but was just the starting gun for a new kind of struggle.

Fresh off the "Train the Trainer" course, riding high on confidence, I was given my first real shot at leadership. I was promoted to New Car Sales Manager.

It was the moment I had worked so hard to earn. Finally, I thought, I would have a chance to put my skills on display and earn my keep. I spent my first couple of weeks drinking from a firehouse, learning the ropes of the desk, how to "pencil" deals, how to use the computer systems, how to pull credit reports, and how to structure a deal so the bank would buy it.

Then they cut me loose to see what I could do.

My first full month running the desk was a success, especially compared to what the department had been doing previously. I felt validated. I felt like I had finally arrived.

But, in a way that only history can repeat, change came knocking again. And this time, it came for me.

Another new management team took over the dealership. They brought their own playbook, and more importantly, they brought their own people. They did not care about my successful month. They had a guy they trusted, a more experienced manager from their previous store.

I was called into the office and told the news: *You are being demoted back to the sales floor.*

I was devastated.

It was not just a change in job title; it was public humiliation. One day I was the boss, approving deals for the sales team; the next day, I was sitting next to them in a cubicle, asking for a pen.

I wanted to quit. I wanted to walk out the door and never look back. The only reason I did not was fear. I was terrified that if I quit, I would prove everyone else right—my dad, the manager who gave me two weeks, the "Old Dogs." They would say, *See? He could not hack it.*

So, I went back to the floor. But I went back different.

My attitude took a major blow. It took weeks for me to get my head on right. But it is amazing how car payments and a mortgage will motivate you to swallow your pride.

I began to sell again, but this time, I entered what I call the "Season of the Mercenary."

With a chip on my shoulder the size of a cinder block, I decided that loyalty was a fool's currency. If they did not care about me, I would not care about them. I became selfish. I was only looking out for Jerry.

Ironically, what I had learned during my short stint as a manager made me a better salesperson than ever before. I knew how the desk worked. I knew how to structure my own deals so they could not say no.

My results were better than ever. I became a machine. I stopped mentoring the new guys; I viewed them as competition. If a manager asked for a favor, I checked my watch. My commission checks became my only reward, and they were big.

Months rolled by. My confidence was slowly returning, built on a foundation of cash and cynicism.

Then the revolving door spun again. Another change in leadership. And this time, they came looking for me.

They needed a manager. They knew I had done it before. They asked me to fill the seat again.

At first, I tried to decline. *Why would I put my head back on the chopping block?* I thought. *I am making good money. I have no headaches.*

But it did not take much convincing. The ego is a hungry animal. With a little encouragement—and a desire to prove once and for all that I belonged in that chair—I accepted.

I became a manager again.

It was not a perfect fit. I did not completely mesh with the culture of that specific leadership team. They were rougher, looser with the rules than I liked. But I managed to get through it. I continued to learn, to grow, and to pay attention. I kept my head down and did the work.

Then came the shift that changed everything.

A new leadership team came in—the "Good Team." This was not just another rotation of car guys. This team brought integrity. They brought excitement. They had a desire to grow the business the right way, mirroring the way Toyota was growing globally.

For the first time in years, I felt a flicker of hope. I respected them. They talked about culture. They talked about volume. They valued the things I valued.

I knew this was where I wanted to be. And, more importantly, they respected me. They saw my numbers. They saw my consistency. They saw that even though I was cynical, I was the most capable guy in the building.

Then the rumor started circulating: The General Sales Manager position is coming available.

The GSM is the captain of the ship. They run the desk, manage the inventory, hire, and fire, and control the flow of every deal. It is the second most powerful position in the store, right under the General Manager.

I knew—I did not think, I *knew*—that the job was mine.

I had tenure. I had a track record. I had survived the demotion, the return to the floor, and the second ascent. I had paid my dues. I had eaten the dirt. Now, it was time for the reward.

I walked around with a quiet swagger. I started mentally redecorating the GSM office. I told Steph, "It's finally happening. All that grinding is about to pay off."

The day of the announcement came. The General Manager called a meeting in the conference room. The air was buzzing. The sales team filed in, whispering. Everyone looked at me. They knew it, too.

The GM stood up. He cleared his throat.

"As you all know," he began, "we have been looking for the right person to lead our sales department to the next level."

I nodded slightly. *That is me.*

"We interviewed a lot of candidates," he continued. "But one stood out above the rest."

I straightened my tie.

"Please join me in welcoming our new General Sales Manager…"

I started to stand up.

"…Ashton."

I froze. I sank back down, the blood draining from my face so fast it made me dizzy.

Ashton?

Ashton was a good guy. A very good guy. He had been the General Sales Manager at the dealership years ago. He was competent. He was nice. He was experienced.

But he was not me.

He had not been in the trenches of *this* store for the last few years. He had not survived the purges. He had not clawed his way back from the demotion. He was an outsider.

The room erupted in polite applause. I clapped my hands that felt like blocks of wood. I pasted a smile on my face that felt like a mask.

I had been passed over.

The meeting ended. I walked out of the conference room, bypassed the showroom, went straight to the bathroom, and locked the door. I stared at myself in the mirror. My face was flushed red.

I was not just disappointed. I was enraged.

This was the second heavy serving of Turnip Greens in my leadership journey, and this batch tasted like poison.

It is unfair, I thought. *It is rigged. It does not matter how hard you work.*

I went back to my desk, but I did not work. I sat there, fuming. Every time I saw Ashton walk by, smiling, shaking hands, sitting in *my* office, a fresh wave of resentment washed over me.

I did not quit. I could not afford to quit. But I decided to make them regret it.

I entered a phase of passive resistance. I did my job, but I did it with a toxicity that leaked out of my pores. If Ashton implemented a new process, I rolled my eyes. If he set a goal, I told the other guys it was impossible. I became a cancer in the locker room.

"He doesn't know what he's doing," I would murmur under my breath. "Just wait. He'll crash and burn just like the rest."

I thought I was punishing them. The truth was, I was only punishing myself. I was carrying around a backpack full of rocks, wondering why I was so tired.

That is when Miss Jessie intervened.

Miss Jessie was the matriarch of our sales floor. She was a woman in her late forties who had only been selling cars a few years but had wisdom beyond any person I had ever met. She did not smoke. She did not curse. She kept a Bible open on her desk next to her prospecting notebook. She was the moral compass that kept the place from sliding completely into darkness.

One hot Tuesday afternoon, the showroom was dead quiet. I was sitting at my desk, aggressively stapling papers, stewing over some minor directive Ashton had given earlier.

Miss Jessie walked over. She did not say anything at first. She just stood there, waiting.

"Hey, Miss Jessie," I grunted.

"Jerry," she said softly. "Walk with me."

We walked to the large glass windows at the front of the showroom, looking out at the rain.

"You're carrying a heavy load, son," she said.

"I'm fine," I lied.

She turned to look at me. Her eyes were kind, but they were sharp.

"You are not fine," she said. "You are angry. You are hurt. And you are letting that root of bitterness grow so deeply that it's going to choke out everything good in your life."

I felt my defenses crumble. "It's unfair, Miss Jessie," I vented. "I earned that seat. I did the work. And they gave it to him."

She listened. She did not interrupt. When I finally ran out of steam, she reached out and patted my arm.

"I know it hurts," she said. "But, Jerry, you are looking at this through the wrong lens. You think you were robbed. But you were protected."

I frowned. "Protected? From a promotion?"

"God's timing is not your timing," she said. "You see the title. You see the money. But you do not see the burden. You need to stop fighting."

"So what am I supposed to do?" I asked. "Just roll over?"

"No," she said. "Psalm 46:10. Be still. You need to trust that God is working, even when you cannot see it. You need to trust that if that door closed, it's because there is a wolf behind it."

I did not want to hear it. I wanted justice, not theology.

"You just watch," she said, walking back toward her desk. "Everything happens for a reason, Jerry. One day you'll understand this is happening *for* you, not *to* you."

I stood there by the window, feeling foolish and furious. *Be still.* It wanted to do nothing. It felt like surrender.

And to a man like me, surrender wanted to lose.

Part 2: The Bullet You Didn't See

"Be still."

I tried. I really did. But for a high-strung car salesperson fueled by caffeine and ambition, being still is physically painful. Finding stillness was as hard as trying to hold my breath underwater.

For the next several months, I watched Ashton run the department. And when I say I watched him, I mean I studied him like a hawk circling a field mouse. I was waiting for him to fail. I wanted vindication. I wanted the "I told you so" moment.

But as the weeks turned into months, my anger began to shift into something else. It shifted into pity.

The dealership, despite the new management's talk of culture, was still a pressure cooker. The ownership was demanding. They wanted growth, and they wanted it yesterday. They managed by spreadsheet, not by reality.

I started noticing the changes in Ashton.

When he first took the job, he was crisp. Sharp suits, high energy, big smile. He shook hands with a firm grip. He talked about his vision for the quarter and all he had hoped to achieve.

Three months in, however, the smile did not seem as bright. He started looking disheveled.

I realized that the "throne" I had wanted was an electric chair.

The demands were impossible. The inventory was short. The market was soft. And because he was the GSM, every single problem landed on his desk. He was the umbrella catching all the acid rain from corporate, trying to keep it off the sales floor.

One Friday evening, late, I was finishing some paperwork. The showroom was empty except for the janitorial crew. I walked past Ashtons's office. The door was cracked open.

He was sitting there with his head in his hands. A picture of his family was on his desk, a wife, and girls. He was staring at it, but he was not smiling. He looked like a man who had forgotten what it felt like to breathe.

I hesitated. Part of me—the bitter part—wanted to keep walking. *He took your job,* that voice whispered. *Let him suffer.*

But the other part of me, the part Miss Jessie was trying to wake up, felt a pang of sympathy.

I knocked on the door frame. "You okay, Ash?"

"Yeah," he said, forcing a smile that looked like a grimace. "Just a long week, Jerry. Just a long week."

I walked away, and for the first time since the promotion, I did not feel envy. I felt relief. I drove home, sat on my couch, and did not think about work for the rest of the night. While I did not know for sure, I would have wagered that Ashton was there until midnight.

The explosion happened just a few months later.

The owner had brought in a consultant to review the business with his team. Three men in expensive suits arrived. They did not look happy.

First, they marched straight into the GM's office. Then they called Ashton in. The blinds were drawn, but the walls were thin.

We could not hear the words, but we could hear the tone. It was loud. It was aggressive. It sounded like a dog fight.

Ten minutes later, the door opened.

Ashton walked out. He was not holding a notebook. He was not holding a pen. He was holding a cardboard box.

The showroom went silent. You could hear the hum of the vending machines.

He did not look at anyone. He walked straight to the front door, pushed it open, and walked out into the heat. He got into his demonstrator vehicle, threw the box in the passenger seat, and peeled out of the lot.

He was gone. Just like that.

I stood there, frozen. I looked at the empty office. The chair was spun around. The phone was off the hook. The picture of his family was gone.

I felt a hand on my shoulder. I turned around. It was Miss Jessie.

She did not say "I told you so." She did not have to. She just looked at me with those knowing, ancient eyes.

"Do you see it now?" she whispered.

I nodded slowly. "I see it."

"The storm that hit him was meant for you," she said. "If you had been in that chair, Jerry, that would be you driving away right now. You would be the one explaining to Steph why you lost your job. You would be the one with the ulcer."

The realization hit me like a physical blow.

The "Passover" was not a rejection. It was a rescue mission.

God had looked at the timeline. He had seen the toxic leadership that was coming down the pipe. He had seen the stress that would have crushed my marriage in its infancy. He had seen that my character was not yet strong enough to handle that level of pressure without breaking.

So, He blocked the door.

He put Ashton in the line of fire to shield me.

I felt a wave of shame wash over me for how I had acted—the anger, the pettiness, the entitlement. I had spent six months cursing the very hand that was protecting me.

I walked into the bathroom—the same bathroom where I had raged six months earlier—and I looked in the mirror again.

"Thank you," I whispered. "I'm sorry I didn't trust You. But thank you."

That day changed how I viewed disappointment forever.

I developed a new theology for my career, one that I call the "Open Hand Policy."

I learned that you can chase a dream, you can work for a goal, but you must hold it with an open hand.

If God puts something in it, you squeeze it tight and steward it well. But if God takes something out of it, or if He refuses to put something in it, you do not make a fist. You do not fight Him for it.

Because if you force a door open that God has shut, you will walk into a room you were never equipped to survive.

The aftermath of Ashton's firing was chaotic, but for me, it was clarifying. I went back to work with a clean heart. The chip on my shoulder was gone, replaced by a quiet gratitude. I started mentoring the younger guys again. I started staying late to help, not for the money, but because it was the right thing to do.

I stopped auditioning for the role and started simply doing the work.

And then, as always happens when you stop striving and start serving, the call came.

It did not come when I was desperate. It came when I was ready.

The team that had been brought in to consult was another new leadership team. Although I remained in my position, the months that followed would prove the most challenging yet. A daily greeting full of swear words followed by toxicity would be a reminder that when you think you have it bad, it can always get worse.

I had been doubted and I had been questioned, but I never could have been prepared for the worst verbal onslaught of threats and degrading comments I had ever endured.

This along with negative publicity that this team created in the small community would soon catch up with our owner and community leader.

Realizing the huge mistake and the toxic culture, ownership cleaned house again. They promoted the General Sales Manager, a man named Levi, to be the General Manager.

Levi respected my work and my passion for Toyota. He knew my strengths and my commitment to the brand, the dealership, and the community.

Shortly after his promotion, he called me into his office.

"Jerry," he said, "I've been looking at the numbers. And I've been looking at the people."

"Yes, sir."

"We need a leader," he said. "Not just a boss. A leader."

I waited. I did not assume anything this time.

"I don't want you to be the New Car Sales Manager," he said.

My heart sank for a split second. *Here we go again.*

"I want you to run the store," he said. "I want you to be the General Sales Manager."

I blinked. "The GSM?"

"You know the operations better than anyone," he said. "You have earned the respect of the floor. And frankly, you've survived enough garbage in this place to prove you have thick skin."

He slid a contract across the desk.

"It's yours if you want it."

I looked at the paper. The title. The salary. The responsibility.

Six months ago, I would have grabbed it with arrogance. I would have thought, *It is about time they recognized my greatness.*

But that day, I picked up the pen with a trembling hand. I felt the weight of it. I thought about Ashton and I thought about Miss Jessie's warning.

I signed it, not with pride, but with humility.

I was ready. Not because I was perfect, but because I had been broken just enough to know that I could not do it alone.

I walked out of that office and looked across the showroom floor. The glass walls of the GM office were behind me. In front of me, the chaos of the car business churned on—salespeople laughing, customers negotiating, phones ringing.

I was the captain now.

But I promised myself one thing: I would not lead like the men who had hurt me. I would not lead with fear. I would not lead with ego.

I would lead with the scars I had earned. I would lead knowing that every person down there was fighting a battle I knew nothing about.

I did not know it yet, but the hardest battles were not behind me. They were just beginning. The dealership would test my skills, but life was about to test my soul.

I was about to enter the "Glass Office." And while the view was great, I would soon learn that glass walls do not just let you see out—they let the heat in.

CHAPTER 4

The Glass Office

Part 1: The Interim King

The road to the top was not a straight line; it was a winding mountain path with switchbacks, falling rocks, and guards at the gate telling me to turn around.

After Ashton's departure, the dealership eventually stabilized for a while under a General Manager named Levi. I was promoted to General Sales Manager (GSM), the role I had been passed over for previously. I held that seat for six months. I ran the desk. I moved the metal. I thought I had found my ceiling.

But in the car business, stability is a myth.

Levi made decisions that did not sit well with ownership. The details do not matter now, but the result was the same as it always was, a sudden vacancy. Levi was out.

Once again, the store was headless.

The owners asked me to step in. Not as the General Manager, but as the "Interim" General Manager. It is a title that means: *Keep the lights on and the doors open while we find the guy we really want.*

I was not offended. In fact, the Toyota District Manager at the time—the corporate liaison who oversaw our region—called me on day one.

"Jerry," he said over the phone, his voice brisk and businesslike, "I want to be clear. You are not going to be the GM. We are looking for someone with more experience. Just hold the fort."

I gripped the receiver. "I understand."

And I did. I was not expecting the crown. I just hoped that when they found the new guy, I could stay on in some capacity. I had been there for years. I had survived the purges. I just wanted to keep my job.

So, I went to work. I ran the store like it was mine, even though I knew it was not.

Then the wind shifted again.

The old District Manager was transferred to another territory. In his place came a man named Scott.

Scott was different. He was young, extremely sharp, and educated. He was not an "Old Dog" with coffee stains on his tie. He had worked in retail, so he knew the grind, but he had also climbed the ranks at Southeast Toyota. He understood the business from a high altitude.

Our owner was a good man, a local businessperson, but he was not a "car guy." He could not teach me about absorption rates, fixed operations, or parts inventory turns.

But Scott could.

Scott offered a wealth of knowledge. He saw that I was hungry—not just for sales, but for understanding the *business*. He sat with me. He walked me through the financial statements. He taught me how the service department feeds the sales department and vice versa.

But Scott was not the only one in my corner.

Inside the dealership, there was a Controller named Stephanie.

We had met in 2005 when she joined the team. At the time, our relationship was not romantic; it was strictly professional. She was the financial backbone of the store. She was sharp, precise, and she did not tolerate nonsense. If my paperwork was sloppy, she sent it back.

But she also saw something in me that I was just starting to see in myself. She saw the work ethic. She saw the way I handled the staff.

After a few months of watching me run the store as the "Interim," Scott saw it too.

Together, Scott and Stephanie petitioned the owners and the powers that be at Southeast Toyota.

"You don't need to hire an outsider," they argued. "You have the guy right here. He just needs some training, some mentorship, and an opportunity."

Mr. Lowe was the first to agree. He must have seen something that gave him peace of mind.

Toyota wasn't as easily convinced. They insisted on having an approved General Manager in the store because Mr. Lowe was an absentee dealer. That meant he wasn't involved in the daily operations of the dealership, and that was concerning to Toyota.

Although it took some convincing, eventually I was given an opportunity: The GM in Training Program.

It was not a handover. It was a gauntlet. For six months, I had to prove I could handle every aspect of the dealership, from the grease of the service bay to the glitz of the showroom. It was grueling. It was exhaustive.

But six months later, I graduated. The "Interim" tag was ripped off my door.

I was the General Manager.

❦❦❦

The office had glass walls.

It was situated just off the showroom floor, elevated slightly, so it felt like I was hovering over the showroom like a captain's bridge overlooking the deck of a battleship.

From my desk, I could see everything. I could see the polished hoods of the new Camrys gleaming under the halogen lights. I could see the salespeople pacing, phones pressed to their ears, hunting for the next deal.

For a kid who started bagging groceries in a white shirt and black tie, this was the mountaintop. It was the title I had chased for over a decade. It came with the salary, the authority, and the respect I had craved since I was nineteen years old.

The first time I sat in that chair as the *official* General Manager, I spun around, looked out at the bustling dealership, and thought, *I made it*.

During this climb, the accolades started piling up. I was not just participating; I was dominating. As the New Car Sales Manager, I had earned the Toyota Sales Excellence Award four years in a row. Later, as General Manager, our team earned the prestigious President's Award for two consecutive years.

Those awards were the gold standard. They meant we were hitting our numbers, but they also meant we were taking care of our customers. I was proud of them. I displayed them. They became the armor I wore to prove I belonged at the top.

But the best thing that happened in those years wasn't an award. It was the evolution of a relationship.

Finding success in relationships while working sixty hours a week is no small task. In the car business, it's not uncommon for people to form deep connections at work. You spend more time there than anywhere else, and sometimes—despite all the warnings and wisdom to the contrary—life unfolds where you least expect it to.

I had been married before and was blessed with a son, Dawson. For a long time, it was just the two of us. We were a team in the truest sense—learning, adapting, and growing together. I didn't know it then, but that team was about to become something much bigger.

Steph and I worked together until 2008. What began as professional respect slowly grew into a genuine friendship. Over time, that friendship deepened in ways neither of us had planned. She saw my ambition, but more importantly, she saw the man behind it. She saw the weight I carried home at night—the stress, the fatigue, the responsibility of trying to be everything at once.

Steph was walking her own path as well. She was a devoted single mother to her son, Bradley, navigating life with the same determination and quiet strength I recognized in myself. Somewhere along the way, two separate worlds began to move closer together. A working relationship became a friendship. A friendship became something deeper. And before we fully realized it, we weren't just thinking about ourselves anymore—we were thinking about how to bring four lives together as one.

Marrying Steph wasn't just the beginning of a new chapter; it was the best thing that ever happened to me. It wasn't about replacing what had been—it was about building something stronger, together. We weren't just blending schedules or households. We were blending hearts, responsibilities, and hopes, creating a family that was chosen, earned, and deeply rooted in love.

She came into my life just as the rocket ship was taking off. She became my anchor in a sea of constant motion. While I was chasing plaques and bonuses, she was building a foundation that—unknown to me at the time—would soon have to support the weight of a collapsing world.

Because here's the thing about mountaintops that no one tells you: the air is thin up there. It is exhilarating, yes. But it is also very, very cold. And you cannot live there forever.

🍎🍎🍎

To understand why the crash happened later, you must understand the armor I was wearing when I took the job.

Years of fighting in the trenches—of being demoted, passed over, and disappointed—had changed me. I was not just ambitious anymore; I was hardened.

I had entered what I now call the "Season of the Fixer."

There is a specific kind of coldness that settles over you when you decide that you are the only person on whom you can rely. After the "Passover" incident with Ashton, I had convinced myself that survival meant self-sufficiency.

I became a transaction machine. I stopped looking at people as souls and started looking at them as resources. *Can this person help me hit the number? If yes, keep them. If no, move them.*

I remember a specific Tuesday during that hardening period. A new hire, a kid who looked just as scared as I had been at nineteen, came up to the glass office. He knocked on the door.

"Boss," he said, "I'm having trouble with this deal. Can you help me?"

The old Jerry, the one who wanted to teach, the one who won the Walkaround Competition, would have pulled up a chair and mentored him.

The General Manager Jerry did not even look up from his spreadsheet.

"Get with the desk," I told him coldly. "I am busy right now. They can give you whatever you need."

He walked away, dejected.

Ten years later, the memory of that moment still stings. I had let my pain make me petty. I had let the pressure turn me into the kind of leader I hated. I was making money, but I was spiritually bankrupt. I was building a kingdom of one.

I tried to do everything myself. I was the first one in and the last one out. I made a rule for myself: *I will never ask anyone to do a job I am not willing to do myself.* That sounds noble, and in some ways, it was, but it was also a trap. It meant I was constantly moving cars, working deals, sweeping floors, and auditing paperwork, terrified that if I stopped moving, the whole thing would collapse.

I did not delegate because I did not trust. And because I did not trust, I was exhausted.

From the outside, I was living the American Dream. I was the young, successful executive running a multi-million-dollar operation. I drove a nice car. I wore nice suits. I had the respect of my peers and the fear of my competitors.

But beneath the surface, the "dream" was slowly turning into a vise grip.

※ ※ ※

The breaking point began with a blessing. Or at least, what we thought was a blessing.

The ownership group approved a massive expansion project. We were going to build a brand-new, state-of-the-art facility.

It was not just a renovation. It was a transformation. We were moving from our old, cramped building into a 72,000-square-foot palace of glass and steel. It was going to be the flagship store for the region. Massive service bays, a luxury waiting area, a showroom that could hold twenty cars.

It was the kind of project most GMs dream of leading. It was a legacy builder.

But for me, it became a second full-time job on top of the one I was already barely surviving.

Suddenly, my days were not about selling cars. They were about blueprints, budgets, and image requirements. I was juggling the daily operations of the existing store, keeping the numbers up so we could pay for the construction—while trying to birth a massive commercial project next door.

To understand the pressure, you must understand the scale.

We were not just putting up a new showroom; we were moving four miles down the street to an entirely new location. Seventy-two-thousand square feet is massive. It involves managing every detail from moving earth to pouring acres of concrete, and making a thousand decisions that all carry a price tag with a lot of zeros.

My life became a blur of red tape. I would start my day early, often walking the construction site with the supervisor, negotiating contracts, and learning to understand a language I never wanted to speak—HVAC loads, zoning variances, fire codes.

There is a specific kind of stress that comes with construction. It is the stress of the "Change Order." You think you have a budget. You think you have a plan. Then the equipment you ordered is unavailable and the only alternative is another $5,000. It is the stress of preparing to open only to find the phone system is not working efficiently or better yet, the city inspector decides the fire lane needs to be six inches wider.

Every delay cost money. And every dollar was scrutinized by the owner.

I remember standing in the middle of the framed-out service drive one July afternoon. The Georgia heat was suffocating—98 degrees with 90 percent humidity. Dust coated my suit shoes. My phone was ringing in my pocket. The sales manager, needing help on a deal. The supervisor was shouting at a subcontractor over the noise of a jackhammer.

I felt a vibration in my chest that had nothing to do with the machinery. It was a flutter. A skip.

It was the vibration of a human being stretched past his tensile strength.

I looked at the steel beams rising against the blue sky. They looked strong. They looked permanent. And for a fleeting second, I envied them. I wished I were made of steel. Instead, I felt like I was made of glass, and someone was throwing rocks.

I was building a monument to the company's success, but I was dismantling my own health brick by brick.

I would leave the construction site, wipe the mud off my shoes, put on my "General Manager smile," and walk into the showroom to lead a sales meeting.

The mental switching costs were exorbitant. One minute I was arguing about ordering shop equipment, the next I was counseling a finance manager on compliance laws. My brain never rested. It could not.

I stopped sleeping. I would wake up at 3 a.m. thinking about light fixtures and interest rates. I stopped eating lunch. I ran on coffee and cortisol. I stopped exercising. I poured every ounce of my vitality into that building.

When we finally cut the ribbon, everyone cheered. It was a beautiful facility. It was a crown jewel. The local news came out. The Mayor shook my hand.

"You did it, Jerry," everyone said. "Look at what you built."

But as I stood there, clapping along with the rest, cutting the red ribbon with the giant ceremonial scissors, I felt hollow.

I had poured myself out, and there was nothing left to refill the vessel. I had built a house for the business, but I had let my own spiritual house fall into total disrepair.

It was a warning shot that I ignored. It taught me that you can be successful at building things and fail at maintaining yourself. And eventually, the cracks in the foundation will show.

And show they did.

Part 2: The Driveway Moment

The noise was deafening. Literally and figuratively.

Even after the construction crews left and the jackhammers stopped, the noise inside my head would not quiet down. I would stand in the middle of that beautiful new showroom, surrounded by the smell of fresh paint and success, and I would feel a tightness in my chest through which I could not breathe.

I was running on fumes. Caffeine and cortisol were the only things keeping me upright.

I started coming home later. It was not always because there was work to do. Sometimes, the work was done by 7 p.m. but I would find reasons to stay. I would reorganize files. I would walk the lot checking for unlocked cars. I would sit in my office and stare at the wall.

Why? Because I was terrified of the quiet.

If I went home, I had to be a father. And I felt like I was failing at both because I had nothing left to give. I was a husk. I had given every ounce of my patience, my energy, and my emotion to the dealership. When I walked through my front door, I was empty.

The breaking point did not happen in a boardroom. It happened in my driveway.

It was a Tuesday night in October. I pulled into the driveway. The neighborhood was silent.

I turned off the ignition of my demo. The engine ticked as it cooled.

I sat there. My hand was on the door handle, but I could not pull it. I could not make my legs move.

I looked at the garage door. Behind it was my life. My real life. The people who loved me not because I was a General Manager, but because I was Jerry. And I could not go inside.

I felt a tear hot on my cheek. Then another.

I looked at my reflection in the rearview mirror. Dark circles under my eyes. Shoulders slumped forward. A face that looked ten years older than the calendar said. I did not recognize the man staring back at me.

Who are you? I asked the reflection.

I was the GM. I was the guy who hit the numbers. I was the guy who built the building.

But take away the title, take away the keys, take away the glass office...and who was left?

I whispered a prayer, but it was not a prayer of faith. It was a prayer of desperation.

"Lord...I don't know who I am anymore."

I realized in that moment that I had become the job. The title "General Manager" had swallowed "Jerry" whole.

My patience was gone. At work, I snapped at people I respected. I micromanaged instead of mentored. I justified it by saying I demanded excellence, but the truth was, I was terrified of losing control. The "Mercenary" instinct from my early years was kicking in again—trust no one, do it yourself, protect the perimeter.

My faith was still there, technically. I went to church when I was not working (which was rare). I prayed over meals. But God felt distant—like a friend I had not called in years because I owed him money. I was not living in grace; I was surviving on grit.

And grit eventually runs out.

I sat in that driveway for what seemed like an hour.

I asked myself a terrifying question: *If I died tonight, right here in this seat, what would my tombstone say?*

The answer came back cold and hard: **He sold a lot of Toyotas.**

The thought terrified me.

Is that it? Is that the sum of life? Units sold? Gross profit generated? Market share captured.

I thought about my two boys. Would they remember me as the dad who played catch, or the dad who was always on the phone? Would Steph remember me as her partner, or as the roommate who paid the bills but was never emotionally present?

I wrestled with it for weeks. Walking away meant leaving a massive salary. It meant leaving the status. It meant walking away from the identity I had spent my entire adult life building.

But the chest pains were getting worse. The anxiety was a constant hum in my ears, like a high-tension wire about to snap.

Finally, I made the decision.

I handed over the keys. I packed the few personal items in my glass office—some pictures and a few awards.

I walked out the glass doors for the last time.

I got into my car in the parking lot, the parking lot of the same dealership that I had arrived at years earlier with so much ambition, where I had won the Walkaround competition, where I had hustled for leases.

I put the car in park, gripped the steering wheel, and cried.

I did not cry from regret. I did not cry from sadness.

I cried from relief.

It felt like someone had cut a hundred-pound weight off my back. For the first time in years, the buzzing in my head stopped.

I was unemployed. I was uncertain. But I was free.

🍎🍎🍎

The months that followed were detox.

Steph and I invested in a small retail venture, something simple, low stakes. We opened a store that had nothing to do with cars. I needed to decompress. I needed to remember what it felt like to be a human being, not a human doing.

We built a life around the simple things. Family dinners. Little League games. Evenings on the porch.

I learned that rest is not laziness; it is stewardship. I had treated my body and my spirit like a rental car—driving it hard, ignoring the maintenance lights, assuming I could just trade it in when it broke. But you do not get a trade-in on your soul.

For a while, the silence was healing. I reconnected with God, not to find leadership but to find Jerry.

I realized we needed steady ground.

So, I did what I knew how to do. I went back to the dealership world.

From 2010 to 2012, I jumped back into the grinder. I worked as a Finance Manager. Then I was promoted to Finance Director. Then I took a role as General Sales Manager at another store.

I thought that after the break, it would be different. I thought I could handle it better this time.

I was wrong.

I found myself once again working in an environment where I felt I did not belong. The hours were long, the culture was cutthroat, and the old familiar weight began to settle back onto my shoulders. I was making money, but I was miserable. I was trading my peace for a paycheck all over again.

It culminated at the end of a particularly brutal week. I had been fighting battles that did not matter, arguing over gross profit, and dealing with the toxicity of the sales floor.

I came home late. I pulled into the garage. I turned off the car, but I did not get out immediately. I just sat there in the dark, listening to the engine tick, feeling the exhaustion in my bones.

Steph came out to the garage. She opened the car door.

I looked at her, and I broke.

"Why does this feel like punishment?" I asked Steph. "I did the right thing. I walked away to save my family and my sanity. But now I feel…stuck."

Steph reached over and took my hand.

"Maybe you're not being punished," she said softly. "Maybe you're being prepared."

"Prepared for what?"

"I don't know," she said. "But God does."

Those words echoed in my head for days. *Prepared, not punished.*

It is easy to trust God when the path is clear. It is hard when you are standing in the hallway, waiting for a door to open.

I started praying a dangerous prayer: *Lord, put me where You want me. Not where the money is. Not where the glory is. Where the purpose is.*

A few weeks later, the phone rang.

It was a recruiter from Prestige, a financial services company in Salt Lake City, Utah. They had found an old résumé of mine—one I had sent months ago and forgotten about.

"We're looking for a Dealer Representative," the woman said. "Someone who knows the car business inside and out, but who understands people. Someone who can go into dealerships and teach them how to do it right. Would you be interested?"

I took the interview.

It was not a GM role. It was not running the show. It was a support role—visiting dealerships, training teams, helping other people succeed. It was a remote position, covering territory in the Atlanta area.

As I listened to the job description, something clicked. This was not about power. It was about influence. It was about taking everything I had learned—the good, the bad, and the burnout—and using it to help others avoid the traps into which I had fallen.

I took the job in March 2012.

Stepping out of the dealership and into the corporate vendor world was a culture shock for which I was not prepared.

For years, I had been the "General Manager." I was the guy everyone came to for answers. I held the keys. I signed the checks. My identity was wrapped up in being the man in charge.

Suddenly, I was a "Rep."

I was not the boss anymore; I was the vendor. I was the guy sitting in the waiting room, holding a bag of donuts, hoping the GM would give me five minutes of his time.

It was a humbling demotion of status, even if it was a promotion in lifestyle.

I remember walking into a dealership in my new territory for the first time. I walked up to the receptionist and asked to see the finance manager.

"They are all busy," she said, barely looking up. "Have a seat."

I sat. And I waited.

Twenty minutes passed. Then thirty. I watched the sales floor, the chaos, the energy—and I felt a pang of longing. I missed the action. I missed the authority. Sitting in that plastic chair, I felt invisible.

My ego took a beating in those early months. I had to learn a new skill set: **influence without authority.**

As a GM, I could tell people what to do. As a Rep, I had to convince them. I had to earn the right to be heard. I had to swallow my pride when a manager half my age brushed me off.

But looking back, that season was crucial. It stripped away the "title" I had been hiding behind. It forced me to develop my personality, my patience, and my ability to listen.

I realized that I had been using my title as a crutch. Without it, I had to relearn how to connect with people simply as Jerry.

It was a quiet season. A humbling season. But it was the season where I learned that my worth was not on my business card.

It was also the season where God moved us geographically.

The territory was in my home state of Georgia, but it required us to relocate to Atlanta. It was an area with which I was not familiar. Fortunately, It was all too familiar for Steph. We moved minutes from her mom and dad. At the time, it seemed like a convenient logistical decision. We wanted to be near the grandparents for the boys.

We did not know then that God was positioning assets before a war.

He knew that in a few years, I would not be able to drive. He knew I would not be able to walk. He knew Steph would need help carrying the load of a dying husband.

If we had not moved—if I had not taken the "step down" to Prestige—we would have been isolated when the storm hit.

As I settled into my role, I really enjoyed my work and really appreciated the company I worked for. It quickly became a new passion. Enough so, that in 2013, I was promoted to AVP. Then, in 2014, to VP. I was climbing again, but this time, I was doing it with balance. I worked from home. I traveled, but I was present when I was home. I coached the boys' teams. I made family a priority.

I felt like I had finally cracked the code. I had escaped the fire, healed from the burnout, and found a sustainable rhythm.

I thought the hard part was over. I thought the "preparation" Steph talked about was for this new career.

I was wrong.

God was not preparing me for a new job. He was not preparing me for a new territory.

He was preparing me for a battle I could not see coming.

It started innocently enough. Just a dull ache in my lower back. I blamed it on the driving. I blamed it on the hotel beds. I blamed it on getting older.

I did not know it then, but the burnout had been a skirmish. The resignation had been a drill. The humbling in the waiting room had been basic training.

The real war was about to begin. And this time, I would not be fighting for a paycheck, a title, or a plaque on the wall.

I would be fighting for my life.

CHAPTER 5

The First Fight

Part 1: The Splinter

It started as nothing more than a nagging ache—a dull, stubborn throb in my lower back that lingered like a splinter I could not reach.

The year was 2018. Life was running on smooth rails. I was six years into my tenure with Prestige, having climbed from Dealer Rep to Assistant Vice President, and then to Vice President. The work was demanding, but I had found a rhythm. I was traveling every few weeks, spending time in the office, attending meetings, and feeling purposeful.

I was forty-something years old. I was a "car guy." I was used to sitting in uncomfortable seats, driving long distances across the Southeast, and carrying the stress of the month's goals in my shoulders. In my mind, back pain was just the tax you paid for a life spent on your feet and playing sports.

I blamed the pain on everything but the truth.

It is the rental car seats, I told myself as I rubbed my lower back after a four-hour drive. *It is the hotel mattresses,* I thought as I tossed and turned in a Homewood Suites in Nashville. *It is just getting older,* I joked to my friends.

I treated the pain like I treated most problems in my life that did not involve a spreadsheet: I ignored it, hoping it would get the hint and leave. I stretched in the mornings. I used heating pads at night. I popped ibuprofen like they were M&Ms.

But the ache did not leave. It got louder. It shifted from a whisper to a shout, a constant, rhythmic reminder that something inside the machine was broken.

Looking back, I realize that pain is often God's way of knocking on the door when we have locked the deadbolt. We try to drown it out with noise and busyness, but the knocking persists because the visitor knows the house is on fire.

One evening after dinner, while working in the yard, I tried to stand up. A bolt of lightning shot up my spine. I grimaced, clutching my knees for support, my knuckles turning white. I could not straighten up. I was stuck in a half-crouch.

Steph was not far away. She stopped and turned around and gave me *that* look. The one that said the debate was over before it began.

"Jerry," she said.

"I'm fine," I grunted, forcing myself upright through the pain. "Just a little sore. I was bent over for too long."

"You are not fine," she said. She did not raise her voice. She did not have to. "You've been complaining about your back for months. You are walking like an old man. You're not sleeping."

"I'll stretch it out," I said, trying to walk to the living room with some sense of dignity. "I have a trip next week. I'll look into it when I get back."

She did not argue. She just shrugged, turned back to what she was doing, and moved on.

I thought I had won the debate. I thought I had dodged the bullet.

I packed my bag. I gritted my teeth through the pain. I got on the plane and went on my trip, doing what I always did—pushing through.

But Steph plays the long game.

She knew that if she argued with me to my face, I would dig my heels in. So, she waited. As soon as I was out of town—while I was sitting in a meeting pretending my back was not on fire—she picked up the phone. She did not ask for my permission; she asked for the chiropractor's availability.

When I got back home a few days later, still wincing every time I moved, she did not ask how I felt. She just handed me a piece of paper with a date and time on it.

"You have an appointment," she said. "Thursday at two."

"I don't want to see a chiropractor," I said.

"I didn't ask," she replied. "You're going."

So, I went—mostly to appease her and prove her wrong so I could get back to work. The chiropractor was a nice guy, confident, with strong hands. He took some X-rays, cracked my back, adjusted my hips, and told me my alignment was off.

"We'll get you straightened out," he said.

I went back for a few sessions. I wanted it to work. I wanted the problem to be mechanical, a bone out of place, a muscle that needed relaxing. Simple problems have simple solutions.

But every time I left his office, the pain was not better. It was sharper. Angrier. It felt deep, like it was radiating from the center of my body rather than the muscles of my back.

Steph did not wait for me to admit defeat. She watched me wince every time I got in and out of the car. She escalated the call.

"If it's your back, let's get a real look at your back," she said. "I'm calling an orthopedic specialist."

I felt relieved going to the orthopedist. I wanted an MRI. I wanted them to find the slipped disc or the herniated vertebrae so we could schedule a surgery, fix it, and get back to my life. I liked problems with clear solutions. *Cut here, stitch there, rehab, done.*

We went in for the scan in December of 2018.

If you have never had an MRI, it is hard to describe the isolation of it.

You walk into a cold, sterile room dominated by a massive, donut-shaped machine. The technician is kind, but they do not stay with you. They retreat behind a glass wall, safe and sound, leaving you alone with the magnet.

I lay down on the narrow table. They handed me a panic button—a small rubber bulb to squeeze if I freaked out. Then they placed a cage-like coil over my chest and slid me into the tunnel.

The ceiling was two inches from my nose. I closed my eyes to keep the claustrophobia at bay.

Then the noise started.

It is not a hum. It is a mechanical assault. *CLANG-CLANG-CLANG. THUMP-THUMP-THUMP.* It sounds like someone is throwing a sledgehammer into a washing machine right next to your head.

"Breathe in…hold it," the voice in the speaker commanded.

You lie there, lungs burning, holding your breath while the machine takes slices of your insides. You try not to move. You try not to think about what the machine might be seeing.

In that tube, stripped of my phone, my watch, my title, and my control, I felt incredibly small.

I tried to distract myself.

The noise was relentless though. It was a reminder that something was happening inside me that I could not see, could not touch, and could not stop.

At the time, I was not worried about anything life-threatening. I was just annoyed by the inconvenience. I was worried about the copay. I was worried about losing a day of work.

I was worried about the wrong things.

A week later, we returned for the results.

I walked into the orthopedic office expecting a prescription for physical therapy or a steroid shot. I was mentally rehearsing how I would tell my boss I might need a few days off for back surgery.

We sat in the exam room. Steph was scrolling on her phone. I was reading a poster about proper lifting techniques.

The door opened.

The doctor walked in. She was not holding a plastic model of a spine. She was not holding a prescription pad. She was holding a manila folder, and she was not looking at my eyes, she was looking at the file.

She sat down on the stool and sighed. It was a small sigh, professional but weary.

"Jerry," she said. "We looked at your spine."

"There is some arthritis, yes," she said. "Some disc compression. That explains some of the stiffness."

I nodded. *Knew it. Getting old.*

"But," she continued, and her voice shifted gears, slowing down, "we found something else. Something that we are more concerned about."

The air in the room went still. The hum of the ventilation system seemed to stop.

"There is a mass," she said.

I blinked. My brain tried to process the word. *Mass?* Like a knot? Like a cramp?

"A mass? On my spine?"

"No," she said. "On your right kidney. It is significant in size—about eight to ten centimeters."

Eight to ten centimeters. I did the mental conversion. That is the size of a softball. Inside me.

"What does that mean?" I asked, though a cold feeling was already spreading through my chest.

"We need to do more imaging," she said, using the careful, hedged language doctors use when they do not want to say the scary word but need you to understand the gravity. "But given the size and the characteristics on the image...we need to rule out renal cell carcinoma."

Carcinoma.

Cancer.

She did not say the word "cancer," but it hung in the air between us, heavy, suffocating, and undeniable.

I looked at Steph. She was frozen, her hand gripping the armrest of the chair so hard her knuckles were white. Her eyes were wide, processing the data, moving from "back pain" to "kidney mass" in the span of three seconds.

"I'm referring you to a urologic oncologist," the doctor said, handing me a piece of paper. "You need to call them today."

We left that office in a daze.

We walked out into the parking lot. The sun was shining. It was a crisp Georgia winter day. Traffic was moving on the street.

How could the world keep spinning?

I got into the truck. I put the key in the ignition, but I did not turn it. I just sat there, staring at the brick wall of the medical building.

I have a mass.

I have a tumor the size of a grapefruit growing on my kidney.

For forty years, I had been the strong one. I was the provider. I was the fixer. I was the guy who carried the load.

Now, I was the patient.

"We're going to figure this out," Steph said, breaking the silence. Her voice was steady, even if her hands were trembling slightly in her lap. "We just take the next step."

"Yeah," I said. "The next step."

I started the truck. I drove us home. But I knew, with a terrifying certainty, that the road I was driving on had just changed direction, and I had no map for where we were going.

This was the first serving of the real Turnip Greens. Not the professional setbacks. Not financial stress. This was mortality. And it tasted bitter.

Part 2: The Illusion of Victory

A urologic oncologist is a surgeon who specializes in cutting bad things out of important places.

We met him a few days later. He was a technician of the human body. He looked at the scans on the lightboard, nodding to himself, measuring angles and density. He did not mince words.

"It's renal cell carcinoma," he said. "Stage 2."

Stage 2.

It sounded serious, but it was not Stage 4. It was contained. It had not spread to the lymph nodes or the blood vessels. It was a rogue agent, acting alone.

"Here is the plan," he said, mapping it out on a piece of paper like a mechanic explaining a transmission repair. "We do a robotic laparoscopic partial nephrectomy. I go in, I cut out the bottom half of the kidney where the tumor is attached, I save the rest of the kidney, and you go on with your life."

"That's it?" I asked. "Cut it out and I'm done?"

"That's the goal," he said. "We caught it early enough. You have an incredibly good prognosis. If we get clean margins, you shouldn't need chemo or radiation."

I felt a rush of adrenaline. *I can do this*, I thought. *It is just a surgery. It is a pothole, not a cliff.*

I was not just being brave; I was relying on experience. I had been down this road before, or so I thought.

Back in 2004, before Steph and I were married, I was a single dad raising my son Dawson and had a run-in with the ER. I had been dealing with a lingering bout of heartburn that would flare up at night. I popped antacids like candy and ignored it. But one night, I woke up with a pain in my chest that felt like an anvil. I had endured pain before, but this was like nothing I had ever experienced.

I grabbed up Dawson, put him in the truck, and took off toward the hospital with the hazard lights flashing. It was not more than a ten-minute ride, but it felt like an eternity. I called my parents on the way to let them know we were headed in, convinced I was having a heart attack.

About two miles from the hospital, a police officer started tailing me. He followed me all the way into the parking lot. As I rolled out of my truck, clutching my chest, he got out and asked if everything was okay.

"No," I gasped.

He helped me inside, where we checked in at the desk. I advised them of my symptoms, and immediately they took me back and started running test after test. X-rays, EKGs, blood work. After a series of tests without finding anything cardiac, an ER doctor came in.

"We're going to give you a GI Cocktail," he advised. "Drink it and let's see what happens."

It was a strange mixture that tasted like Mylanta mixed with Lidocaine. I drank it. Within two minutes, things started improving. The anvil lifted. Feeling confident, the ER released me shortly after with a cocktail for the road, just in case I needed it, and an appointment for an ultrasound.

Two days later, I returned, and it was determined that my gallbladder had stopped working and would need to be removed. Surgery was scheduled a few weeks later. It was outpatient. The surgery was microscopic—laparoscopic—with four small incisions in my abdomen.

I recovered quickly from that surgery. I was back to work in just a few days. I remember thinking, *Modern medicine is amazing. Surgery is easy.*

So, sitting in the oncologist's office in 2019, hearing the words "robotic" and "laparoscopic," I mentally filed this away as "The Gallbladder 2.0." I thought I would be sore for the weekend and back to selling cars on Monday.

Boy, was I wrong.

As I sat there feeling confident, the surgeon paused. He took off his glasses and looked at me.

"But, Jerry, there is one thing."

"What?"

"You smoke."

"Yes."

"Not anymore," he said. His voice was not a suggestion; it was a command. "Kidney cancer thrives in smokers. It restricts blood flow, which hurts recovery. If you want to keep living, you stop. Now."

I had smoked for years. I enjoyed it. It was my stress relief. It was my pause button during a stressful deal or a long drive. But looking at the gray-scale image of the mass growing inside me, the cigarettes suddenly did not look like relief. They looked like bullets.

I walked out of that office on Friday and smoked my last cigarette Sunday night.

I remember that moment vividly. It was not a ceremony. There was no fanfare. It was February 11, 2019.

I sat in my garage, looking at the pack. For years, those white cylinders had been my crutch. They were my companions in the solitude of leadership. But looking at them in the shadow of the doctor's office, they did not look like friends anymore. They looked like thieves.

I realized that every puff I had taken over the years was a loan against a future I now desperately wanted to see.

The air was crisp—February in Georgia can still have a bite to it. I did not light one for "old time's sake." I did not mourn the loss. I crushed the pack in my hand. The sound of the crinkling foil and paper felt satisfying, like the first punch in a fight I was determined to win.

I tossed it into the trash can by the curb.

That date is etched in my mind, not just because I quit a habit, but because it was the first time I truly chose life over lifestyle.

The physical withdrawal in the days that followed was real—the irritability, the reaching for a pocket that was empty—but my mind had shifted. Every time a craving hit, I visualized the mass on the scan. I visualized the surgeon's face.

I told myself: *You are not a smoker anymore. You are a fighter.*

That decision was the first step of my preparation. Before the surgeon ever picked up a scalpel, I had already started the work of cutting cancer out of my life. It taught me that while I could not control the tumor, I could control the terrain it lived in. And I was going to make my body a hostile environment for anything trying to kill me.

The surgery was scheduled for February 27, 2019.

The two weeks leading up to it were a strange mix of anxiety and surprising peace. I was scared, yes. I worried about the anesthesia. I worried about complications. I worried about leaving Steph alone if things went wrong on the table.

But I also felt surrounded. Our friends rallied. Our family prayed and checked on us constantly.

On the morning of the surgery, we arrived at the hospital before the sun came up. Hospitals have a distinct smell at 5 a.m.—floor wax and fear. It is quiet, but it is a busy kind of quiet.

Pastor Kelly met us in the parking garage with a basket and a prayer.

"Lord," he prayed, "guide the surgeon's hands. Steady Jerry's heart. Let him know that You are already in the operating room waiting for him."

We checked in, then we waited. One by one, family appeared. My parents, in-laws, sisters, and a good friend named David Creamer stopped by to give their support and to help pass the time.

Eventually, they called us back. I changed into a gown that never closes quite right. Nurses bustled around, starting IVs, checking vitals, asking me to repeat my name and date of birth a dozen times.

I looked at Steph. She was smiling that brave smile she uses when she is terrified but trying to be strong for me.

"I love you," I said. "See you on the other side."

"I'll be right here," she whispered. "I'm not going anywhere."

The operating room was bright and cold. It looked more like a spaceship than a medical bay. The robot arms—the Da Vinci system—loomed over the table like a giant metallic spider. It was intimidating but also reassuring. Technology was on my side.

The anesthesiologist placed a mask over my face. "Take a deep breath," he said. "Think of somewhere nice. Think of the beach."

I thought of the porch. I thought of Steph.

Then, the world went black.

❦❦❦

Waking up was violent.

Usually, in movies, people wake up from surgery groggy and peaceful. I woke up feeling like a truck was parked on my chest.

The pain in my side was immeasurable—a roaring fire, a sharp, hot agony that radiated through my entire torso. I tried to talk, but only a gasp came out. The room was spinning. Machines were beeping frantically—*beep-beep-beep-beep*.

"His pressure is spiking," someone shouted. "We can't get it down."

The nurses tried to calm me. They pushed meds. They told me to relax. But the pain was too loud, and the panic was setting in. Nothing they did worked.

Finally, a nurse said, "Get his wife. Bring her back here."

A moment later, Steph was there. She leaned over the rail, her face close to mine.

"I can't breathe," I gasped, gripping the sheets. "I can't breathe."

"You can breathe," she said, her voice firm but gentle, cutting through the noise in my head. "Jerry, look at me. You must calm down. You have to take it easy."

I tried to focus on her eyes.

"Your blood pressure is too high," she said. "They won't let you go to your room until it comes down. You need to breathe. Just breathe."

Her voice was the only thing that was anchoring me to the bed. Slowly, with her coaching me through every inhale and exhale, the panic began to recede, even if the pain did not.

It took hours. It felt like an eternity of fighting my own body, but eventually, the numbers on the monitor stabilized enough for them to move me.

They wheeled me out of recovery. I was exhausted, drifting in and out of consciousness. As they rolled me into the hospital room, I looked around, expecting Steph to be right there waiting for me.

The room was empty.

"Where is she?" I asked the transport nurse.

"I'm not sure," she said, locking the wheels of the bed. "She should be here."

Panic started to rise again. I could not move my body without agony, but I needed to find her. I reached out, my hand shaking, and fumbled for the room phone on the bedside table. I struggled to hit the buttons, my vision blurry, but I managed to dial her cell number.

She answered on the first ring.

"Where are you?" I rasped.

"I'm in the waiting room," she said. "Have they moved you?"

"I'm in the room," I said. "I'm all alone."

"I'm coming," she said, and the line went dead.

No one had told her. The staff had moved me without updating her.

Within minutes, she burst through the door. She was out of breath, her face flushed. She rushed to the side of the bed and grabbed my hand.

"I'm here," she said. "I'm right here. I didn't know they moved you."

Finally, with her hand in mine, the room stopped spinning.

I was alive.

The surgeon came in later, looking tired but pleased. He was still wearing his scrubs.

"It went perfectly," he said. "We got the tumor. Margins are clear. You kept more of the kidney than I expected. You're going to be fine."

We got it.

The words washed over me like cool water.

The recovery was brutal. Every cough felt like my stitches were tearing. Every movement was a negotiation with pain.

But every time I woke up and saw the drainage tube or felt the sting of the incision, I reminded myself: *It is gone. The cancer is gone.*

I went home a few days later. Steph turned our living room into a recovery suite. I slept sitting up for weeks, surrounded by a fortress of pillows because lying flat was impossible. I could not lift anything heavier than a milk jug. I walked like an old man, shuffling down the hallway, holding the wall for balance.

But I was happy.

I was a survivor.

I had faced the beast and won. I had the scars to prove it. I had four one-inch lines on my side that marked the battlefield.

I went back to work a few weeks later and as spring turned into summer, I started traveling again. I told my story to anyone who would listen—how God had saved me, how the doctors were heroes, how I was living proof of the power of prayer and early detection.

I felt invincible. I thought I had eaten my Turnip Greens. I had swallowed the bitter taste of fear and surgery, and now I was ready for the dessert. I was ready for the rest of my life.

I went in for my six-month follow-up scan in late September. I was not even nervous. I treated it like a victory lap. I joked with the technicians. I planned where Steph and I would go for dinner afterward to celebrate.

The following week, I flew to Utah for work with Prestige. I was back in the rhythm of business, feeling strong, feeling like the cancer was a distant memory.

While I was on the road, my phone pinged. The results were available in the patient app. I opened the notification with high confidence, expecting to see the words "No evidence of disease."

But as I scrolled through the radiology report, I stopped. There were words in the notes I was not expecting.

"Sub-centimeter pulmonary nodules, bilaterally and Right hilar lymphadenopathy with mild mediastinal lymphadenopathy."

I stared at the screen. I did not know what *lymphadenopathy* meant, but I knew enough to know that "bilateral pulmonary nodules" meant spots on both lungs. And right below that, there was a line that made my stomach drop: *Recommendation to follow up.*

Something seemed off. If everything was clear, why was there a recommendation for follow-up?

Anxiously, I called the oncologist's office from my hotel room and left a message. I waited. One day passed. Then two.

It would be a few days before I finally got a return call. When the nurse finally spoke to me, her tone was casual, almost dismissive.

"Everything is okay, Mr. Herrin," she said. "The doctor reviewed it. If there was a problem, we would have notified you immediately. Those notes are just standard observations."

Feeling unsure, I accepted their answer. I wanted to believe them. I wanted to believe that I was just being paranoid, that I was overreacting to medical jargon I did not understand.

I hung up the phone and tried to focus on work. I moved on.

But I would not settle with that as a final answer.

I did not know it then, but the book was not finished. The enemy had not surrendered; it had just gone underground.

I thought I had fought the fight of my life.

But I was wrong. That was just the warm-up. The real war was gathering its forces, and it was coming for my lungs.

CHAPTER 6

The Call

Peace is a fragile thing. It is beautiful, but it is brittle.

For six months, I had lived in the warm, comforting glow of "cancer-free." The surgery was behind me. The scars on my abdomen were fading from angry red to a dull pink. I had quit smoking, changed my diet, and convinced myself that the partial nephrectomy was just a speed bump in a long, healthy life.

I tried desperately to hold onto the nurse's words, *everything is okay*—and lock the worry away in a drawer in the back of my mind.

But while my mind was trying to accept the "all clear," my body was raising the alarm.

It started with my breath.

I noticed that the stairs in my house felt steeper. I would walk to the bedroom and feel winded, like I had just run a sprint. I would carry a suitcase across a parking lot and would need to stop to catch my wind, pretending to check my phone so no one would notice I was gasping.

I told myself it was just deconditioning. *I am recovering*, I thought. *I spent weeks in a chair. I am just out of shape. I need to hit the treadmill.*

I went back to my life. I did not pray about it. I did not stress about it. I tried to forget about it.

But the breathlessness did not forget me. It got worse. A dull ache started in my chest, a heaviness that sleep could not cure.

In October 2019, I had a routine physical scheduled with my primary care physician. He was the kind of doctor who did not just read the summary; he read every line. He knew my history. He knew about the kidney.

I walked in, feeling mostly fine, but tired. I sat on the crinkly paper.

"How are you feeling, Jerry?" he asked.

"Good," I lied. "A little winded sometimes. But good."

He listened to my chest with his stethoscope for a long time. Longer than usual. He moved the cold metal disc around, frowning.

"I want to see that report from your surgeon," he said.

I handed him the paperwork I had brought with me. He read it in silence. The room was quiet, save for the ticking of the clock on the wall.

He stopped reading. He looked up at me.

He shook his head slowly. "I don't like this, Jerry," he said quietly. "I would like to take another look."

"The surgeon said it was fine," I offered, trying to defend the peace I had built.

"Maybe," The doctor said. "But I want to be sure. Surgeons look at where they cut. I look at the whole patient. Let us order a dedicated chest CT. Today. Just to be safe."

I agreed, mostly to humor him. I went for scans a few days later and then went on about my daily life. I told myself he was just being overcautious.

The call came on December 12, 2019.

It was a Thursday morning. Steph and I were getting ready for the day. Coffee was brewing. The news was playing softly in the background. It was a perfectly ordinary morning in the Herrin household.

The phone rang. Steph answered.

I watched her face change. It was not a dramatic gasp; it was a subtle draining of color. Her eyes locked onto mine, wide and terrified. She did not say a word, just handed me the phone.

"This is Amber," the voice said.

"Hey, Amber. How are you?"

"The doctor would like to see you today."

My stomach dropped. "Today? I have a full schedule. I am supposed to fly out tomorrow. Can it wait until next week?"

There was a pause. A heavy, pregnant pause.

"No, Jerry," she said firmly. "He wants to see you *now*."

Now.

That word hung in the air like a guillotine blade. Doctors do not clear their schedules for good news. They do not demand you come in "now" to tell you everything is fine. They do not interrupt your life unless your life is in danger.

I hung up the phone. The room felt suddenly cold.

"We have to go," I told Steph.

We drove an hour and a half to his office in silence. The radio was off. The world outside the windows looked the same—cars merging, billboards flashing, people rushing to jobs that suddenly seemed so trivial—but inside our car, the air was thick with unspoken fear.

When we arrived, there was no waiting. Amber met us at the door. She did not smile. She did not ask about the drive. She led us straight back to Exam Room 3.

We sat there, holding hands, gripping so tight my knuckles turned white. I stared at the anatomical chart on the wall—lungs, heart, veins. I tried to breathe, but the air felt thin.

The door opened.

The doctor walked in holding the folder. He did not sit behind the desk; he pulled a rolling stool up in front of us, knee to knee. He looked tired. He looked like a man who hated this part of his job more than anything else.

He took a deep breath. He looked me in the eye.

"Jerry," he said gently. "The scans came back."

I nodded. *Just say it.*

"The cancer is back."

I felt Steph flinch beside me.

"And," he continued, "it has metastasized. It's in your lungs."

The room spun.

"My lungs?" I whispered.

"Yes. Multiple nodules. It is widespread. It's Stage 4."

Stage 4.

The number echoed in my head. Stage 1 is a scare. Stage 2 is a battle. Stage 4 is a sentence.

I stopped hearing him for a moment. His voice became a muffled hum, like I was underwater. I stared at the diploma on the wall behind him. *University of…somewhere.* I counted the edges of the frame. *One, two, three, four.* I focused on the dust on the baseboards. I focused on anything but the reality that was crashing down on me.

I felt like I had been punched in the gut. I looked at Steph. She was crying silently, tears streaming down her face, but she had not let go of my hand.

"There is no cure," he said softly.

We weren't naive. We didn't have the luxury of thinking, *Maybe it won't be that bad.*

We knew exactly what this beast looked like. Back in 2010, we lost my sister-in-law, Robin, to pancreatic cancer. We had sat in the waiting rooms. We had seen the devastation it left behind. We had watched the toll it took on a family—the slow, agonizing theft of a person you love.

So, when the doctor said, "Stage 4," I didn't just hear a medical term. I saw the ghost of that pain. I saw the destruction we had already lived through, and the terrifying thought that it was coming for our house next.

"So, what's next? What do we do now?" I asked, my voice cracking.

"We treat it. We treat for time. We treat for quality of life. There are new drugs, immunotherapies. But you need an oncologist immediately."

We walked out of that office into the blinding afternoon sun. It felt violent. How could the sun shine? How could the birds sing? Didn't the world know that the clock had just started ticking?

We got into the car. I did not start the engine. I just stared at the steering wheel, my hands trembling.

She reached over, grabbed my face with both hands, and turned me to look at her. Her eyes were full of tears, but there was fire behind them.

"We've got this and we'll get through this together," she said. "It is *not* the end. You are not a statistic, Jerry. You are my husband. And we are not doing this alone."

She pulled me into her, and I finally broke. I wept in the parking lot of the doctor's office, grieving the life I thought I was going to have.

CHAPTER 7

The Chair

Part 1: The Cocktail

We had a diagnosis. Now, we needed a battle plan.

The doctor had given us the "what," Stage 4 Renal Cell Carcinoma. But he could not give us the "how." For that, we needed a specialist. We were referred to an oncologist who specialized in kidney cancer.

If my primary care doctor was the scout who spotted the fire, my Oncologist was the fire chief holding the hose.

He was a calm man with steady eyes and a demeanor that suggested he had seen everything a human body could do to destroy itself, and he was not intimidated. He sat us down in his office, which was cluttered with medical journals and files, and laid out the reality of the situation.

"We can't cut this out," he explained, pointing to the imaging on his screen. The white spots on my lungs looked like stars in the night sky, but they were not beautiful. They were invaders. "It's in the blood. It is system wide. We must treat the whole system."

When you are staring at a Stage 4 diagnosis, phrases like "standard of care" do not sound very reassuring. Standard of care means "what we usually do." But I did not want usual. I did not want average results. I wanted a miracle. I wanted the nuclear option.

Ultimately, we were presented with a choice.

"Option A," he said, "is the standard immunotherapy. It boosts your body's immune system to fight cancer cells. It has a decent success rate."

"And Option B?" I asked.

"Option B is a clinical trial," he said. "It's called COSMIC-313."

He slid a packet of paperwork across the desk. It was thick enough to be a novel.

"It's a Phase 3 trial," he explained. "We take the standard immunotherapy—the current best option—and we combine it with a new oral chemotherapy drug called Cabozantinib. It cuts off the blood supply to the tumors. It starves them."

"What's the catch?" Steph asked. She was already reading the fine print.

"It's a randomized, triple-blind study," he said. "That means you get immunotherapy for sure. But for the pill…you might get Cabozantinib, or you might get a placebo. Neither you, nor I, nor the nurses will know which one you are taking."

It was a gamble. Joining a trial meant more tests, stricter protocols, more blood draws, and the uncertainty of being a guinea pig for science. It meant surrendering even more control to a system I did not fully understand.

We took the paperwork home. We sat at the kitchen table that night, staring at the list of potential side effects. It was a parade of horrors ranging from high blood pressure and hair loss to organ failure and "hand-foot syndrome."

"Why would I do this?" I asked, rubbing my temples. "Why not just take the proven path? Why risk getting a placebo?"

"Because the proven path might not be enough," Steph said softly. She was reading the survival statistics for standard care. They were not great.

Then I remembered something that my oncologist had said, as an afterthought.

"Jerry, even if this does not help you, the data we get from your participation could help get this drug approved. It could save the life of a man who gets diagnosed five years from now."

That struck a chord in me. It vibrated against the leadership principles I had spent twenty years teaching. *Service. Legacy. Planting trees under which you will never sit.*

The idea that my fight could be useful to someone else changed the equation. It gave the suffering a purpose before it even began. I was not just a patient; I was a pioneer. I was walking into the unknown so that the path might be clearer for the guy coming behind me.

I looked at Steph. "Let's do it."

"You're sure?"

"If I'm going to fight," I said, "give me the heavy artillery. And if I go down, let my data help someone else win."

We signed the papers.

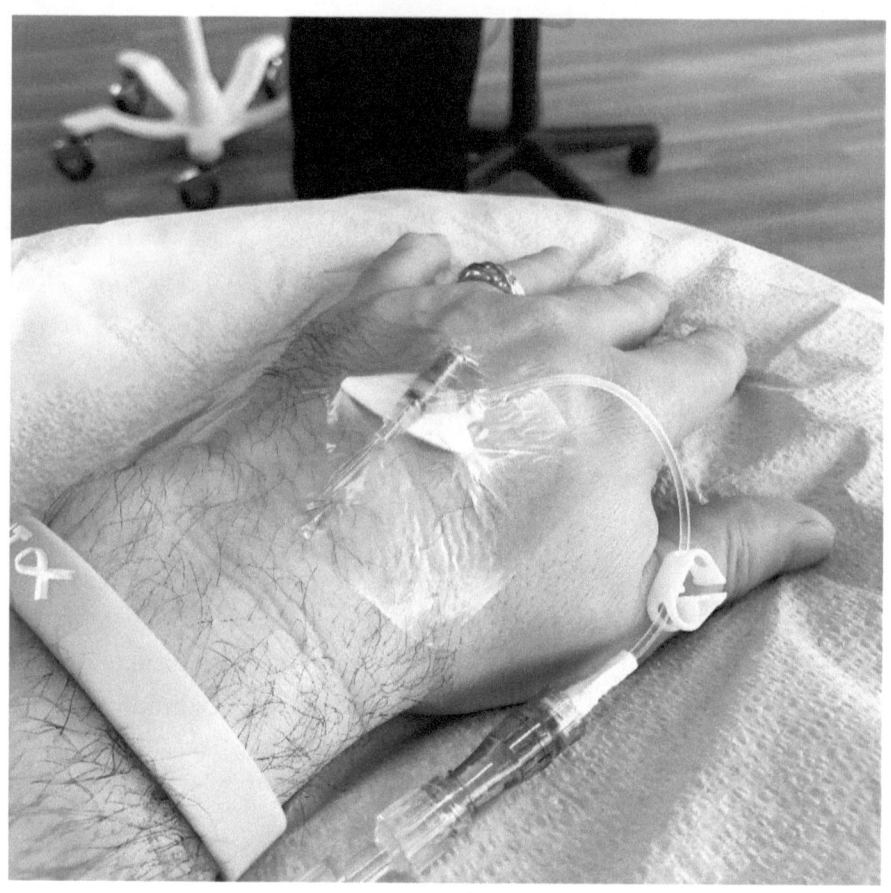

Treatment began on January 24, 2020.

I remember walking into the infusion center for the first time. I expected it to look like a dungeon—dark, depressing, filled with people at the end of their ropes. I expected it to smell like death.

Instead, sunlight spilled through large floor-to-ceiling windows. The room was bright. There were televisions playing daytime talk shows—*The Price Is Right*, *The View*. Nurses in colorful scrubs moved efficiently between rows of large vinyl recliners.

It did not look like a place of death. It looked like an airport terminal where everyone was waiting for a flight they did not want to take.

We checked in at the front desk. I was given a plastic wristband with my name and date of birth—a shackle that would become a permanent accessory for the next year.

"Herrin, Jerry M. DOB: XX/XX/XXXX."

"Right this way, Mr. Herrin," she said. "Pick a chair. Any chair. The ones by the window are popular, but you can pick any open chair that you would like."

I chose a recliner that allowed me the best view of the city.

I sat back, assuming the IV would be the easy part. A quick pinch, a piece of tape, and we would be done.

I was wrong. I had failed to plan. I had not drunk enough water, and my veins were flat, dehydrated, and hiding.

The nurse tapped my arm, frowned, and tried. Nothing. She tried again. Nothing. She called for backup. A second nurse came over, studying my arm like a map with no roads. It took five attempts—five stinging jabs—before they finally found a line that held.

It would prove to be a continual battle every time I arrived. The nurses always wanted to start the IV in my forearm, but my veins refused to cooperate. We usually had to settle for the back of my hand—which stung—or the fold of my elbow, which eventually became my personal choice just to get it over with.

Finally, with the line taped down and my arm throbbing, she hung the bags on the IV stand.

"This might feel cold," she warned.

I watched the clear liquid drip from the bag, snake down the plastic tube, and disappear into my arm. It was a strange psychological hurdle to clear—willingly letting someone pump toxic chemicals into your veins in hopes that they would kill the thing trying to kill you.

Poison to kill the poison.

Steph sat beside me in a guest chair, trying to keep a semblance of normalcy, but I saw her eyes darting to the IV bag every few seconds, counting the drips.

"Are you okay?" she asked for the tenth time.

"I'm okay," I lied.

My stomach was churning. My head was spinning with anxiety. But I was not going to say that. I felt that if I gave the sickness a name—nausea, fear, pain—I was giving it power. So, I stayed silent.

The infusion took about two hours. It is a slow process. You cannot rush the chemistry.

As the hours ticked by, I began to observe the room. The infusion center is a unique society. It has no hierarchy.

In the outside world, we were different. There were CEOs and plumbers in that room. There were grandmothers and teenagers. There were people wearing Gucci loafers and people wearing work boots covered in mud.

But in "The Chair," we were all the same.

We were all tethered to poles. We were all tired. And we were all bargaining with God for more time.

By the time the bag was empty, I felt drained. Physically, I felt heavy. Mentally, I felt like I had run a marathon.

The nurse came back to unhook me. "You did great," she said. "See you next time."

It felt like a sentencing.

Steph drove us home. I leaned my head against the cool glass of the window, watching the trees blur by. I felt the medicine seemingly moving through me in a strange, metallic type of sensation.

I closed my eyes.

One down, I thought. *God knows how many to go.*

🍎🍎🍎

The side effects did not hit immediately. They crept in like a fog over the next few days.

First, fatigue. It was not like being tired after a long day at the dealership. It was not sleepiness. It was a cellular exhaustion. It felt like gravity had tripled. My limbs felt like they were made of lead. Walking from the bedroom to the kitchen to get a glass of water, felt like climbing Everest. I would have to sit down halfway there to catch my breath.

Then came the taste.

They call it dysgeusia. I called it "Metal Mouth." Everything I ate tasted like I was chewing on aluminum foil. My favorite foods—steak, coffee, even my favorite, a Salted Caramel Mocha Frappuccino—tasted industrial. Water tasted like pennies.

Food became fuel, nothing more. The joy of eating—one of life's simplest pleasures—was gone. I ate because I had to, forcing down bland calories just to keep the engine running.

Then came the pill.

Whether it was the placebo or the real Cabozantinib, something was happening. My hair thinned. My skin started to change.

But the hardest part of those first few months was not the physical symptoms. It was the mental game.

When you start a new treatment, you are in limbo. You are taking the medicine, suffering the side effects, but you do not know if it is working. You must wait three months for the first scan.

Three months of trusting the process without seeing progress.

It requires a level of faith that feels impossible. You are walking in the dark, hoping there is a floor beneath your feet.

I tried to work. I tried to be normal. But "normal" was gone.

I was living in two worlds. In one world, I was Jerry the VP, answering emails and taking conference calls. In the other world, I was Jerry, the Stage 4 Cancer Patient, monitoring my blood pressure logs and wondering if the cough I had was the cancer growing or just allergies.

It was a lonely time. But it was about to get lonelier.

Because just as I was getting used to the rhythm of the Chair, the world outside the window began to fall apart.

It was March of 2020. And a new word was about to enter our vocabulary.

Covid.

Part 2: The Silent War

If waiting is hard, waiting alone is agonizing.

In early March of 2020, just as I was beginning to understand the rhythm of this fight, just as I was getting used to the nurses and the comforting presence of Steph sitting beside me—the world outside our windows changed.

A new word entered the lexicon. *Pandemic.*

COVID-19 swept across the country like a grass fire in a drought. It shut down businesses. It emptied highways. It turned neighbors into strangers. For most people, the lockdown was an inconvenience. It meant working from the kitchen table, baking sourdough bread, and missing sports on TV.

For a Stage 4 cancer patient, it was a siege.

I was already fighting a war on the inside. My immune system was compromised, occupied with the battle against tumors in my lungs. Suddenly, the air itself became a threat. The stakes, which were already life-and-death, somehow got higher. If I contracted the virus, it would not just be an illness; it would be a death sentence. Furthermore, testing positive meant I would be paused from the clinical trial, the very lifeline that was keeping me alive.

We did not just have to fight cancer; we had to hide from the world.

I remember the day the hospital policy changed. It was a shift that severed the one physical comfort I had come to rely on during treatment: Steph's presence.

We pulled up to the cancer center for my infusion. It was a routine we had established together. Steph gathered her bag, ready to come in, sit beside me, and be the second set of ears I desperately needed. She was my advocate, my note-taker, my hand-holder.

But after our typical visit with the doctor, we were stopped.

"Patients only," the staff member said, her voice muffled behind a mask and face shield. She held up a hand. "No visitors allowed past this point. No exceptions."

The reality of those words hit us hard. We had done every step of this journey together. From the first back pain to the surgery to the devastation in the doctor's office, we had been a unit. *Team Hterrin*.

Now, I had to walk into the fire alone.

We hugged by the entrance, and she reminded me that she would be out in the car waiting. It felt wrong, like being deployed into combat without your partner.

"I'm not leaving the lot. Keep your phone on. Text me when you get seated and when you are finished."

Everyone was masked. There were no smiles, no small talk, no shared nods of encouragement. Just eyes darting nervously above surgical masks, everyone afraid that the person next to them might be the carrier that ended their fight.

I walked into the infusion room. It had changed. The curtains were drawn between chairs. The communal snack basket was gone.

I sat in the same leather recliner by the window, hooked up to the IV, and looked at the empty guest seat beside me.

That empty chair screamed.

It amplified the vulnerability I felt. For the first time, I could not lean on Steph's strength when the fatigue hit. I could not squeeze her hand when the anxiety spiked. I was alone with the drip.

I pulled out my phone and sent Steph a text to let her know we were about to get started.

I looked out the window. Knowing she was just on the other side of that wall gave me a tether to reality. She sat in that parking lot for hours, every single time, refusing to drive away, just so she could be as close to me as the rules allowed. She worked in the car, making phone calls, checking emails, whatever was needed. She ate her lunch in the car. She prayed in the car.

Back inside, stripped of the "props" of faith, the church gatherings, the hugs from friends, the physical presence of my wife, I found something else. I found a raw, unfiltered dependency on God. There was no one else in the infusion room to talk to. No distractions. Just me and Him.

🍒🍒🍒

It was on one of those drives home early in the treatment cycle that the fear nearly broke me.

The reality of the situation was settling in. I was Stage 4. I was pumped full of chemicals. A deadly virus was shutting down the world outside. The anxiety was at its peak, a constant hum in my chest that made it hard to breathe.

Steph was driving. She always drove on treatment days because the meds made me a bit tired. I was in the passenger seat, staring out the window, watching the Georgia landscape roll by but seeing nothing. I was describing my fear to her, pouring out the "what-ifs" that had been plaguing me in the infusion chair.

What if this does not work? What if I leave you alone? What if I run out of time?

The radio was playing low in the background, just white noise under our conversation.

Then the song changed.

It was not a hymn. It was not a worship song. It was "Live for Today" by the eighties rock band Ratt.

I stopped talking. I listened to the lyrics cutting through the static:

"Live for today…do not wait until tomorrow. Wasting your time being somewhere you do not want to be. Rely on faith to get you through your sorrow. Nothing can stand in your way so live for today."

It was purely coincidental. A random algorithm on a classic rock station. But it hit me like a ton of bricks.

I sat up straighter. The fog of anxiety that had been choking me for weeks suddenly lifted, just enough for me to see clearly.

I turned and looked at Steph. Her hands were steady on the wheel.

"Steph," I said, my voice clearer than it had been all day. "I can't die every day."

She glanced at me. "What?"

"I will only die once," I said. "That day is going to come whenever God decides it comes. But until then, I cannot spend every single day dying. I can't spend my time worrying about something I have zero control over."

I looked back out the windshield. The world looked different. It did not look like the place I was leaving; it looked like a place I was still living in.

"I need to spend my time living," I told her. "I need to make the most out of the days I do have. Because if I spend today worrying about dying tomorrow, I lose both days."

That moment in the car became the turning point of my mental battle. It did not cure cancer, but it cured the paralysis. It gave me a mantra that I would repeat to myself every time the dark thoughts tried to creep back in: *You only die once. Do not do it today.*

☙☙☙

I needed that mantra, because while my mind was finding its footing, my body was entering a tailspin.

The immunotherapy was doing its job—it was revving up my immune system to hunt cancer. But the immune system is a blunt instrument. It does not always distinguish between the good guys and the bad guys. In its fury to kill the tumors, it turned its sights on my thyroid.

The thyroid is the engine of the body. It controls your metabolism, your energy, your temperature, your weight. It is the primary thermostat. And the treatment broke it.

First came the storm.

My thyroid went into overdrive (hyperthyroidism). It dumped hormones into my system like someone holding down the accelerator on a parked car. I felt wired, anxious, and jittery, my heart racing while I was sitting still. I could not sleep. I felt like I was vibrating.

Then came the crash.

After burning hot, my thyroid simply gave up. It stopped producing hormones completely. I swung from hyperthyroidism to hypothyroidism—and then to nothing.

This was a challenge that rivaled the cancer itself.

The fatigue changed from "tired" to "paralyzed." It was not just that I did not *want* to get up; it was that I physically could not keep my head up.

I was still trying to work. I was on conference calls, trying to lead my team, trying to be the VP. But I would be sitting at my desk, listening to a report, and my chin would hit my chest. It felt as though my energy had suddenly drained away. I would snap awake, terrified that I had missed something, terrified that someone had noticed.

Then came the weight.

Because my metabolism had shut down, my body started hoarding everything. I was not eating more—in fact, I had lost my appetite to a degree—but I was blowing up.

I gained thirty pounds in a matter of weeks.

I did not recognize myself in the mirror. My face was puffy ("moon face," they called it). My clothes did not fit. I looked swollen and sluggish. I felt like a stranger in my own skin.

It was a biological rollercoaster. One day I was freezing, wrapped in blankets in a heated house. The next day I was sweating. My emotions were volatile.

I remember looking at Steph one afternoon, feeling the weight of the extra pounds and the fog in my brain, and saying, "I don't know who I am right now. I don't feel like Jerry."

"You're still Jerry," she said, her voice steady as always. "Your body is simply confused. We have to help it."

We had to manage the unmanageable. We had to adjust medications, monitor levels, and ride out the storm until the doctors could get my hormone levels synthetic and stable.

It was the dark season. The cancer was the enemy I could see on a scan, but the thyroid issue was the enemy I felt every second of every day. It stole my energy. It stole my focus. It tried to steal my identity.

But even in that fog, I held onto the Ratt song. *I cannot die every day.*

I could not control my thyroid. I could not control the weight gain. But I could control my outlook. I could choose to wake up, even if I fell asleep an hour later. I could choose to keep working, even if I had to stand up to stay awake.

☙☙☙

By late March of 2020, I had three rounds of infusions behind me. The world was in full lockdown. But in our house, the only statistic that mattered was about to be revealed.

It was time for the first post-treatment scans.

This is the moment every cancer patient dreads. "Scanxiety." You have taken the poison. You have endured the thyroid crash. You have prayed the prayers. Now, science tells you if it was worth it.

We sat in the doctor's office.

The wait felt longer than usual. Every time a door opened in the hallway, I jumped.

Finally, he walked in. He was not holding the folder close to his chest this time. He was holding it open.

And he was smiling behind his mask. I could see it in his eyes.

"Good news, Jerry," he said.

The air rushed back into the room.

"The tumors in the lungs are shrinking," he said, pointing to the images on his screen. He swiveled the monitor so I could see. "See this spot here? It was 1.8 centimeters. Now it is 1.2. And this one? Gone completely."

I stared at the black and white shapes. I did not know how to read a CT scan, but I knew what "gone" meant.

"And," he added, "there is no new growth. Stable disease in the kidney bed. Significant reduction in the lungs."

Shrinking.

It meant time. It meant the gamble on the clinical trial had paid off. It meant the thyroid struggle, the weight gain, the fatigue—it was all worth it.

"It's remarkable," he said. "You're responding better than we hoped. The combination is working."

I walked out of the cancer center that day, and even though I was thirty pounds heavier and exhausted, I felt lighter than air.

I was not cured. I still had months, years, of treatment ahead. I was still Stage 4. The road was still long.

But I was winning.

That night, we celebrated with a simple dinner. I still did not have much of an appetite, but whatever it was may have been the best meal of my life.

I looked around the table at my family. The boys were laughing at a video on their phone. Steph was smiling, really smiling, for the first time in months.

I realized then that the "Chair" had not just been a place of treatment. It had been a place of transformation.

It had stripped me of my vanity. It had stripped me of my illusion of strength. It had messed with my metabolism and my mind. But it had replaced those things with something far more durable.

Endurance.

I had walked into the fire, and I had not burned up.

I went to bed that night, closed my eyes, and prayed a new prayer.

Lord, I do not know how long this road is. But I know You're walking it with me. And if I have breath, I will keep sitting in that chair.

I fell asleep instantly. For the first time in a long time, I did not dream about cancer. I dreamed about living.

CHAPTER 8

Steph's Song

Part 1: The General and the Gatekeeper

There is a specific, heavy kind of loneliness that comes with being the patient. You are the center of a solar system of worry, and sometimes, that gravity feels crushing. You are the one with the plastic wristband that chafes your skin. You are the one with the port scar on your chest. You are the one everyone asks about in hushed tones. *How is Jerry? Is Jerry tired? Is Jerry eating?* You feel the weight of their concern, and you feel the pressure to be okay for them, to perform wellness even when you feel broken.

But there is another kind of loneliness, even heavier, that comes with being the caregiver.

The caregiver does not get the sympathy card; they get the workload. They must be the nurse, the pharmacist, the chauffeur, the chef, the insurance negotiator, and the cheerleader. They must hold the bucket when the nausea hits, and then they must go downstairs and make dinner for the kids as if the world is not falling apart. They must absorb the fear of the person they love most in the world, while having no place to put their own.

For the last few chapters, I have told my story. I have told you about my pain, my fear, and my faith. But if I stopped there, I would be telling a lie. Because this is not just my story. I was the one in the bed, but Steph was the one making the bed. I was the one fighting the disease, but she was the one fighting for me.

If my life is a song—a melody of highs and lows, of loud crashing cymbals and quiet pauses—then Steph is the rhythm section. She is the bassline. She is the steady, thumping beat that holds the whole chaotic mess together so the rest of us do not spin out of control.

To understand Steph's role in my survival, you must understand who she was long before the cancer arrived. You must understand the professional before you can appreciate the partner.

I respected Stephanie professionally before I loved her romantically. We met in 2005, back in the dealership world. In the automotive industry, the sales floor is often a chaotic, testosterone-fueled environment. It is loud. It is aggressive. It is a place where egos run rampant and the loudest voice usually wins.

But Steph was the Controller. In a dealership, the Controller is the financial backbone. They are the keeper of the keys, the guardian of the assets, and the final word on compliance. It is a role that requires immense precision and an iron backbone.

I watched her lead in that environment for years. I saw how she handled the pressure. When a sales manager would try to push a deal through that was not right—the paperwork was sloppy, or the margins were fudged—Steph would stop it. She would not yell. She would not make a scene. She would simply slide the folder back across the desk and say, "Fix it."

She did not lead through fear; she led through competence. She commanded respect because she was right, and she was fair. In a business where people are often treated as disposable commodities, Steph treated everyone with dignity, but she held them to a standard of excellence.

I admired that about her. I wanted to emulate that quiet strength. I saw a leader who understood that you get the best out of people not by squeezing them, but by supporting them and holding them accountable. She was calm in the center of the dealership storm.

When we got married in 2009, I thought I knew how strong she was. I thought I knew the depth of her character. But you do not really know the strength of a foundation until the earthquake hits.

When the earthquake came, the Stage 4 diagnosis, I went into shock. I am a "fixer" by nature. I am a person of action. If there is a problem, I want to attack it. I want to kick down doors, make phone calls, and demand answers. I operate on speed and volume.

But you cannot intimidate cancer. You cannot negotiate with a tumor. You cannot "close" a diagnosis. For the first time in my life, my toolkit was empty. I was paralyzed.

Steph did not try to fix it. She simply stabilized us.

She went into warrior mode. But not the kind of warrior who charges into battle screaming with a sword drawn. She was the strategic General sitting in the tent, looking at the map, moving the pieces. She realized immediately that this was not a sprint; it was a siege. And to survive a siege, you need a system.

She became the Vault.

She did not carry a physical notebook, but she did not need to. Her mind became a steel trap for the logistics of my survival. She memorized the medication schedule like it was her own heartbeat. She knew exactly which pills had to be taken with food and which I could take on an empty stomach. She knew the half-life of the immunotherapy drugs. She knew the difference between a "tired" sigh and a "pain" sigh before I even realized I was making a sound.

If you have never fought cancer in the American medical system, you cannot understand the administrative violence of it. Fighting the disease is only half the battle; the other half is fighting bureaucracy. The approvals, the denials, the copays, the "out of network" surprises, the endless hold music. It is designed to wear you down.

Steph took that burden completely off my shoulders. She became the CEO of my care.

I would see her sitting at the kitchen table, phone pressed to her ear, or stirring a pot on the stove with her free hand, managing a conference call with an insurance adjuster. Her voice would be calm, firm, and relentless. She never lost her cool. She never screamed. She just waited them out. She knew the policies better than the representatives on the phone. She fought for me in cubicles and call centers I never even saw, winning battles over CPT codes and authorization numbers so that I could focus on simply breathing.

She managed our entire household infrastructure without dropping a single ball. The bills got paid. The boys got to school. The groceries appeared in the fridge. She created an environment of normalcy in the middle of a crisis. To the outside world, the Herrin household was running smoothly. Inside, she was holding up the walls with her bare hands.

But her role went beyond medical manager. She also became the Gatekeeper.

When you are sick, especially with something as serious as Stage 4 cancer, people want to help. They mean well. They love you. They want to visit. They want to call. They want to hear the update.

How are the scans? How is he feeling? What did the doctor say? Is the treatment working?

But here is the truth that no one tells you: when you are the patient, talking is exhausting. Retelling the story of your latest scan wants to relive the trauma. Answering the question "How are you?" is a minefield. Do you tell the truth—*I feel like I have been run over by a truck, and I'm terrified I won't see Christmas*—or do you lie and say, *I'm hanging in there,* just to make them feel better?

Steph saw this. She saw how my energy drained away after a ten-minute phone call. She saw how I would slump in the chair after trying to be upbeat for a visitor. She saw the "performance" of being the brave cancer patient wearing me thin.

So, she stepped in front of me. She became the filter.

She absorbed the weight of the world, so I did not have to. She took the texts. She fielded the calls. She politely told people, "Jerry is resting today, but I will tell him you called." She updated the family so I would not have to repeat the same medical details five times a day.

I realized later just how much she must have deflected—the well-meaning questions, the unsolicited advice, the emotional concern of friends and family. She carried the burden of communication so that I could save my limited energy for healing.

There were times I knew she was handling things I never even saw. She created a kind of quiet space around me, a sanctuary where I did not have to perform or explain myself. I could just be. If I wanted to sit in silence, she sat in silence. If I wanted to talk about football to distract myself, she talked about football.

She protected my peace with a quiet ferocity.

I realized that while the doctors were treating my body, Steph was curating my environment. She ensured that the stress stopped at the door, allowing our home to remain a place of rest rather than a command center for crisis.

Even during the height of COVID, when she was forced to wait in the parking lot during my infusions, that sense of protection remained. I knew she was out there, just on the other side of the brick wall, handling whatever needed to be handled. She was the perimeter guard.

She created a bubble. Inside the bubble, there was only faith, rest, and healing. Outside the bubble was the noise. And she stood at the perimeter, arms crossed, ensuring the noise stayed where it belonged.

She did all of this while working her own job, while being a mother to our sons, and while managing her own fear that she might lose her husband. She never asked for credit. She never asked for a break. She just showed up, every single day, and led our family through the valley of the shadow of death.

Part 2: The Anchor of Faith

If faith was the foundation of my survival, Steph was the fortress that protected it.

To understand how we survived the spiritual mental game of Stage 4 cancer, you must understand that not all faith looks the same. Faith has different personalities, different rhythms, and different breaking points.

My faith tends to be what I call "Rollercoaster Faith." I am an emotional person. I feel things deeply. When I see a miracle—a good scan, a pain-free day, a moment of clarity—I am on the mountaintop. I am shouting "Hallelujah" and ready to charge hell with a water pistol. I feel God's presence like a physical weight.

But when I see a shadow—a bad number on a lab report, a new ache in my chest, a look of concern on a doctor's face, I slide into the valley. I wrestle. I question. I bargain. I look for signs. I am like Thomas in the Upper Room; I need to see the wounds to believe the resurrection. I need to see the wind move the trees to know it is blowing.

Steph has "Knowing Faith."

She does not need to see the wind. She rests in the character of God, not the circumstances of the day. She understands that just because it is raining does not mean the sun has ceased to exist; it just means there are clouds in the way, and clouds are temporary.

Throughout the long, grinding months of the clinical trial, there were inevitably days when doubt crept in. The adrenaline of the initial fight had worn off, and we were left with the monotony of the battle. The timeline felt too long. The progress felt too slow. The side effects were relentless.

In those moments, my mind would spiral. I would play out the worst-case scenarios in my head in 4K resolution. I would convince myself that the plan was failing, that the medicine had stopped working, that I was running out of time. I would sit in my recliner, staring at the ceiling fan, feeling the cold grip of despair tightening around my chest.

But Steph never spiraled with me.

She became the Anchor. When I would voice my fears—*What if this is not working? What if we are running out of options? What if I leave you with a mortgage and a funeral?* She would not engage with the panic. She would not argue the statistics or try to offer empty platitudes about "positive thinking."

She would simply hold her ground.

She carried quiet confidence that was baffling to me at the time. It was not that she was in denial about the cancer; she knew exactly how high the stakes were. She read the same reports I did. She knew the survival rates. But she had access to a reservoir of peace that I could not reach.

She did not try to manipulate the outcome; she aligned herself with the One controlling the outcome.

I remember finding her on the back porch one morning during a particularly low week. The sun was coming up through the Georgia pines, the air heavy with humidity. She was just sitting there, her hands wrapped around a mug of coffee, looking into the woods.

I sat down next to her, heavy with worry. "I don't know if I have enough faith for this," I admitted. "I'm trying to believe, Steph. But I am tired. I'm just so tired."

She turned to me. Her eyes were clear. There was no panic in them.

"You don't have to have enough faith right now," she said. "I have enough for both of us."

She was not being arrogant. She was being factual. She was telling me that in a marriage, faith is a shared resource. When one person's tank is empty, the other person's tank can run the engine.

There were times when I was too weak—physically depleted by the thyroid crash or spiritually drained by the fear—to believe for myself. I was tapped out. I could not pray. I could not hope.

In those moments, she believed for me.

There is a story in the Gospels, in the second chapter of Mark, that sums up exactly what Steph did for me during those two and a half years. It is the story of the paralyzed man.

This man could not walk. He could not move. He was dead weight. He heard that Jesus was in Capernaum, teaching in a house, but he had no way to get there. He could not crawl. He could not fight the crowd.

So, four of his friends picked him up. They carried him on his mat. When they got to the house, the crowd was so thick they could not get in the door. Most people would have given up. Most people would have said, "Well, we tried. Maybe next time."

But these friends were relentless. They climbed up the side of the house, dragging their friend with them. They dug a hole through the roof—through clay and tiles—and lowered the man down right in front of Jesus.

The scripture says something fascinating in verse 5: *'When Jesus saw **their** faith, he said to the paralyzed man, 'Son, your sins are forgiven.'"*

It does not say Jesus saw the *man's* faith. The man might not have had any faith left. He was paralyzed. He was helpless. He was just lying there, staring at the hole in the ceiling, wondering if he was about to be dropped.

Jesus saw *their* faith. Friends' faith. The faith of the people holding the ropes. The faith of the people who refused to let the obstacle be the end of the story.

Steph was the friend on the roof.

She carried my mat. When I was paralyzed by doubt, when I could not move, when I could not find the words to pray because the fear was choking me, her faith was the thing that lowered me into the room with Grace.

She dug through the roof of my despair with her bare hands. She held the ropes when my grip failed. She presented me to God daily, hourly, saying, *"Here he is. I know You can heal him. I am not letting go until You do."*

I often wonder about the mechanics of faith—how it works, and why it works. God honors that kind of intercession. He looks at the people standing in the gap and moves mountains because of *their* trust. I am alive today because of the medicine, yes. But I am also alive because my wife held the rope.

We often talk about "finding the right person" in marriage. We look for compatibility, for chemistry, for shared interests. We want someone who likes the same movies, laughs at the same jokes, and wants the same kind of vacation.

But you do not marry someone for the good days. You marry them for the bad ones. You marry the person you want to be in a foxhole with when the shells start falling.

I look back at the timeline of our lives—the "coincidences" that brought us together in 2005, the years working side-by-side at the dealership, the friendship that turned into love, the move to Atlanta—and I see the Signature of God written in bold ink.

He knew.

He knew that in 2019, I would need a partner who did not panic. He knew I would need a woman who could stare down a Stage 4 diagnosis and not blink.

If I had married a woman like me—someone who needed to control everything, someone who rode the emotional highs and lows, someone who needed constant reassurance—we would have imploded. We would have fed each other's anxiety until it consumed us both. We would have spun out.

But Steph is the water to my fire. She does not extinguish me; she contains me. She keeps me from burning the house down. She cools the heat of my fear so that I can think clearly again.

Her faith was not loud. She did not run around quoting scripture verses at me when I was in pain. She did not wear her spirituality on her sleeve. It was deeper than that. It was foundational. It was the bedrock that the rest of our house stood on.

In the middle of the night, when the "what-ifs" woke me up. *What if the cancer spreads to the brain? What if the treatment stops working?* I would reach out and touch her arm. She would be asleep, breathing steadily. And just feeling that steadiness would calm my own heart.

I would think, *If she is not panicking, I do not need to panic either. If she trusts God this much, I can borrow some of that trust.*

She modeled a posture of surrender that I was desperately trying to learn. While I was trying to be the General Manager of my cancer, she was being the Daughter of the King. She knew her Father had it under control, so she did not have to micromanage the miracle.

That is the Anchor of Faith. It does not mean you do not feel the storm; it means you do not drift. It means you stay put. And because she held fast, I did not drift away either.

Part 3: The Rhythm of Grace

As I began to recover—as the scans cleared, the thyroid levels stabilized, and the "second chance" shifted from a desperate hope to a daily reality—I started to notice something about Steph.

For two and a half years, she had been running on high-octane adrenaline. She had been operating in a state of sustained "Code Red." When you are in the middle of the war, you do not feel the weight of the armor. You just wear it because you must. You march. You fight. You survive.

But when the war ends, or at least when the ceasefire is called, the adrenaline fades. And when the adrenaline leaves, the exhaustion rushes in to fill the void.

I started to see the toll the journey had taken on her. It was not a dramatic collapse. Steph is not the type to fall apart; she is the type to endure. She is the type to keep standing until the last dish is washed and the last light is turned off. But I saw it in the quiet moments.

I saw it in the way she would sit on the couch in the evenings, staring at the television but not really watching it, her mind clearly somewhere else. I saw it in the way she moved a little slower in the mornings. The sparkle in her eyes, usually so bright and mischievous, was dimmed by a fatigue that sleep could not touch. She had been holding her breath for thirty months.

I realized that while I had been fighting for my life, she had been fighting for our future. And she had been doing it while carrying the terror that she might have to live that future alone.

It was my turn.

For two and a half years, she had served me. She had been the protector, the driver, the gatekeeper, the prayer warrior, the chef, and the nurse. She had put her own needs, her own fears, her own desires, and her own life on a high shelf to ensure that I survived. She had made her world small so that mine could keep spinning.

Now, I needed to serve her.

I realized that "healing" was not about my kidneys or my lungs. It was about healing the balance of our partnership. You cannot have a healthy marriage if one person is always the giver and the other is always the taker. That dynamic, born of necessity during illness, becomes toxic if it lingers in health.

I started looking for ways to give back the care she had poured out. It started with small, practical things. As my strength returned, I took over the kitchen. I wanted her to come home to a meal, not another chore. I took over the logistics of the house so she could unclench her mind.

But more importantly, I wanted to give her back her identity.

For so long, she had been "The Cancer Wife." She had been the caregiver. I wanted her to remember that she was Stephanie—the woman with dreams, with a sharp wit, with a love for travel and adventure.

I remembered something she had told me years ago, before the sickness stole our timeline. She had said, *"I just want to experience life. I want to go to warm places and see sights I've never seen."*

So, we started planning. We did not just plan doctor appointments anymore; we planned life. We booked trips. We prioritized the experiences she had put on hold. I wanted to show her that the life she fought so hard to save was going to be a life worth living for *her*, too.

Recovering our marriage was a deliberate process. Trauma changes a relationship. It creates a groove, a habit of interaction where every conversation revolves around health, symptoms, and schedules.

Did you take your pill? How is your energy? When is the next scan?

We had to break that loop. We had to learn how to be husband and wife again, not just patient and case manager. We had to relearn the rhythm of intimacy and friendship.

We had to relearn laughter. Real laughter—not the dark gallows humor of the hospital, but the light, easy laughter of two people who enjoy each other's company. We had to relearn how to talk about things that did not matter—movies, politics, the neighbors—because the luxury of talking about trivial things is one of the greatest gifts of health.

I remember one evening, sitting at dinner. I started to give her a report on my day—my energy levels, my appetite, the usual medical update.

She listened, but I could see she was distant.

I stopped. "I'm doing it again," I said.

"Doing what?"

"Making it about me. About cancer."

I reached across the table and took her hand.

"How was *your* day?" I asked. "Not your day managing me. Your day being you."

She smiled, and it reached her eyes. "It was good," she said. And she told me about a funny interaction at the store, about a book she was reading, about a thought she had.

It was a simple conversation. But it felt like a victory. It felt like we were reclaiming the territory the disease had stolen.

Steph challenged my leadership, too. She did not just comfort me; she sharpened me.

As I returned to work and began to navigate the "Kingmaker" phase of my career, she was my sounding board. She reminded me that the greatest impact I could have was not in building a business, but in building people.

She would watch me on the phone, mentoring a young manager or talking a colleague through a crisis. She would bring me a glass of water and sit nearby.

"You know you're not getting paid for that, right?" she would tease gently.

"I know," I would say.

"Good," she would reply. "Because that's the best work you do."

She understood the currency of legacy better than I did. She knew that my survival was not an accident; it was an assignment. And she encouraged me to walk in it.

She often reminded me, *"You lead best when you love most. People follow authenticity more than authority."*

Because of her, I stopped chasing titles and started chasing impact. I realized that if I wanted to be half the leader she was in our home, I had to serve my people with the same selflessness she showed me.

If my life is a song, Steph is the melody. Without her, it is just noise. She is the reason the song kept playing when the world tried to silence it. She provided the rhythm of grace that allowed me to keep walking when I could not see the path.

To the wives, husbands, and partners walking through the fire with someone they love: I see you.

I see the lonely nights you spend staring at the ceiling, praying for a miracle while the person next to you sleeps. I see the tears you hide in the shower so your family will not worry. I see the fatigue you wear like a heavy coat that you never take off.

I see the notebook you keep in your mind, the mental spreadsheet of pills, appointments, and insurance codes. I see the brave face you put on for the kids, the way you tell them, "Everything is going to be okay" even when you are not sure it is true.

You are the unsung heroes. You do not get the "survivor" T-shirt. You do not get to ring the bell at the infusion center. The doctors do not high-five you.

But you are the reason the bell gets rung.

Your love is the medicine that doctors cannot prescribe. Your presence is the therapy that insurance does not cover. You are the hands and feet of God in the darkest rooms. You are the anchor that keeps the ship from drifting out to sea.

And to Steph: Thank you.

Thank you for holding the pen when my hand was shaking too hard to write. Thank you for believing in the sunrise when I was convinced it was always going to be night. Thank you for loving me not just for who I was—the successful provider—but for who I became—the broken, rebuilding man.

You taught me that love is not a feeling; it is a verb. It is staying. It is fighting. It is enduring.

We ate the Turnip Greens together. We swallowed the bitter parts of life side by side. We tasted fear, uncertainty, and pain.

But because we ate the greens, we got strength.

And now, sitting here on the other side, watching the sun go down over the life we built, riding in the golf cart with the wind in our faces...

Baby, the grace sure tastes sweet.

CHAPTER 9

Surrender vs. Control

Part 1: The General Manager of Cancer

The most dangerous lie I ever believed was that I was in control.

For forty-something years, I built my life on the premise that if I worked hard enough, planned smart enough, and anticipated the curves in the road, I could steer the car exactly where I wanted it to go.

In the car business, control is the currency. You control the deal structure. You control the inventory. You control the conversation. If a month started slowly, you did not pray about it; you worked late, called more leads, and forced the numbers to bend to your will.

I was a "fixer." That was my identity. If there was a problem, Jerry fixed it. If sales were down, I fixed it. If a building needed to be built, I fixed it.

But cancer does not care about your work ethic. It does not care about your negotiation skills. You cannot outwork a tumor. You cannot "manage" metastasis.

After the initial rush of treatment began—the scheduling, the insurance approvals, the chemo appointments—the adrenaline started to fade. The logistics were settled. The plan was in motion. And suddenly, I was left with the one thing a man like me hates most:

Stillness.

The frantic activity of "fighting" the disease gave way to the crushing reality of living with it. I was doing everything the doctors said. I was taking the meds. I was showing up. But the outcome remained terrifyingly out of my hands.

So, I did what I always did. I tried to become the General Manager of my own survival.

I attacked cancer like it was a failing dealership. I did not buy books on philosophy or memoirs of survival. I looked for data. I wanted the hard numbers.

I scoured the internet until my eyes burned at 2 a.m. I read medical journals I did not fully understand, trying to decode the language of oncology. I was not just looking for hope; I was looking for proof.

Specifically, I was obsessed with the "double-blind" nature of the trial. I drove myself crazy trying to figure out if I was taking the real Cabozantinib or the placebo. I analyzed every twinge in my body. *Is this rash a side effect of the drug? If it is, that means I am getting the real thing. If I do not feel sick today, does that mean I am taking a sugar pill?*

I tracked my vitals religiously. I obsessed over things that did not matter, like exact hydration levels, because they were the only variables I could control. I was trying to outsmart the trial. I was trying to predict the score before the game was over.

I told myself I was being proactive. I told myself I was being a "good patient."

But Steph saw the truth.

One evening, she found me at the kitchen table, buried in my phone. I was studying lab results, cross-referencing them with articles on COSMIC-313, scrolling through forums where other patients discussed their symptoms. I was rubbing my temples, trying to find a correlation between my blood pressure spikes and the medication schedule.

She put her hand on my leg.

"Honey," she said softly. "Stop."

I looked up, defensive. "I'm just looking at the data. I need to stay on top of this. If I can figure out the side effect profile, I'll know if the drug is working."

"You're not organizing," she said. "You're gripping. You're trying to drive the bus from the back seat."

I leaned back, exhausted. The tension in my neck was so tight it felt like a steel cable. "If I don't drive, who will? I must do something, Steph. I can't just sit here and not know."

"You know Who is driving," she said. "But you have to take your hands off the wheel first. You're exhausting yourself trying to do God's job."

I resented her comment in that moment. *God's job?* I thought. *God is not the one with the tumors. God is not the one swallowing the pills.*

But deep down, I knew she was right. I was trying to manipulate an outcome that was completely beyond my reach. I was trying to use human logic to solve a spiritual problem.

☙☙☙

Surrender is a beautiful word in church. We sing about it. *I surrender all.* It sounds peaceful, holy, and serene. We raise our hands and close our eyes, and it feels nice.

But in real life, surrender wants to die.

It wants to give up. It wants to admit you are weak. For a man who prided himself on strength, on being the provider, on being the guy who made things happen, surrender did not feel like an act of faith; it felt like an act of failure.

But God has a way of breaking you down to build you up. He knows exactly how much weight the beam can hold before it snaps, and He was loading the wagon.

The breaking point did not happen in a hospital. It did not happen in the infusion chair. It happened on a Tuesday afternoon in my backyard.

I was feeling well enough to go for a walk, just a short loop around the property to get some fresh air. It was a beautiful Georgia day, the kind where the humidity breaks and the pines smell sharp and clean. The sky was blue. The birds were singing. It was the kind of day that makes you glad to be alive, which made the fear of dying that much sharper.

I was walking, but my mind was not on the trees. It was on the "what-ifs." The vultures were circling.

What if I am on the placebo? What if I cannot go back to work full-time? What if we run out of money? What if I become a burden to Steph?

The anxiety swelled in my chest, tighter, until I could not walk anymore. It felt like a physical hand squeezing my lungs.

I stopped by an old tree at the edge of the yard. I just needed to stop moving.

I leaned against the rough bark. My legs gave out. I slid down the trunk until I was sitting in the dirt.

I was tired. Not just chemo tired. Soul-tired.

I was tired of trying to be positive. Tired of trying to be strong for my boys. Tired of investigating every symptom. I was tired of managing cancer.

I closed my eyes. And finally, I admitted the truth I had been hiding from everyone, including myself.

"I can't fix this," I whispered.

The words hung in the air.

"I can't fix this."

I waited for the panic to set in. I expected to feel hopeless. I expected the ground to open.

But instead, as the admission settled over me, I felt something else.

Relief.

It was as if I had been holding up a collapsing wall with my bare hands for months, muscles screaming, veins popping, terrified that if I let go, the roof would cave in on my family. And suddenly, I realized the wall was not mine to hold. It never had been.

I stayed there in the dirt for a while. I did not get up immediately. I let the realization wash over me.

I spoke to God—not with the polished prayers I used at the dinner table, but with raw, unedited honesty.

"God, I am angry," I said aloud. "I am scared. And I do not understand why this is happening. I tried to live right. I tried to work hard. This feels like punishment."

That was the root of it. Deep down, a part of me believed that cancer was a consequence. I failed some cosmic test. That if I had been a better Christian, a better husband, or a better man, this would not be happening. I was treating God like a vending machine—*I put in the good works, where is my blessing?*

But in the quiet of that afternoon, I felt a shift. It was not an audible voice—I have never heard God speak like a man speaks—but it was a thought so clear and contrary to my own that I knew it was not from me.

This is not punishment, Jerry. It is preparation.

I sat with that word. *Preparation.*

Preparation for what?

I did not know. But the shift from "victim" to "student" changed everything. If this was punishment, I was helpless. I was just serving time. But if this was preparation, then there was a purpose. If God was preparing me, then He intended for me to have a future to use it.

I unclenched my fists. I physically opened my hands and let them rest on my knees, palms up.

"Okay," I said. "You drive. I'll ride."

☙☙☙

Surrender did not change my circumstances overnight. I still had cancer. I still had appointments. I still had the side effects.

But it changed the atmosphere of my heart.

The next morning, I woke up, and the familiar rush of anxiety hit me—the mental checklist of worries. *Did I take the pill? What is my blood pressure?*

But this time, I had a weapon.

I surrender this, I thought.

It became a daily discipline. A rhythm.

When I worried about the medical bills: *I surrender this.* When I worried about the pain in my foot: *I surrender this.* When I worried about the timeline: *I surrender this.*

I realized that surrendering is not a one-time event. You do not just sign a contract with God and walk away.

Surrender is a daily, hourly decision to give back the control you tried to steal while you were sleeping.

It changed how I prayed.

Before, my prayers were a list of demands. A strategic plan I wanted God to sign off on. *Heal me. Fix this. Change that.*

Now, my prayers became questions. *What are You teaching me? Who can I encourage today? How can I represent You in this waiting room?*

The shift from "Why me?" to "What now?" is the most powerful pivot a human being can make.

"Why me?" keeps you looking backward, searching for blame. It traps you in the past. "What now?" turns you forward. It looks for opportunity. It invites God into the mess.

Once I stopped trying to be the General Manager of my cancer, I became a better patient. I became a better husband.

I stopped hiding my fear from Steph. I let her see the weak days. I stopped trying to protect her from the reality of my condition. And surprisingly, our marriage did not crumble under the weight; it got stronger. Vulnerability is the glue that holds relationships together, and for years, my pride had kept me from being truly vulnerable.

Now, I had no pride left. And we were closer than ever.

But surrender is not about giving up control; it is about finding a new kind of confidence. A confidence that is not based on your ability to fix the problem, but on God's ability to sustain you through it.

I developed a new framework for my thinking. I call it the "Even If" theology.

Part 2: The Theology of the Furnace

There is a paradox in faith: When you are weak, then you are strong.

I used to think that it was just poetic language. It sounds nice on a greeting card. It sounds noble in a sermon. But I lived it. And living it feels vastly different than reading it.

Physically, I was weaker than I had ever been. The treatment was doing its job on the tumors, but it was also waging war on my muscles. There were days I needed help getting out of a chair. There were days I could not open a water bottle. My physical strength, the strength I had used to build displays, walk car lots, and carry my children, was gone.

But spiritually? I was becoming iron.

The things that used to rattle me—a rude comment, a traffic jam, a financial hiccup, a delayed flight—did not even register on my radar anymore. When you are trusting God for your very breath, you stop worrying about whether the barista got your order wrong. You stop worrying about who got the credit in the meeting.

I found peace that did not make sense. The Bible calls it the "peace that passes understanding." Logic said I should be a wreck. Logic said I should be depressed, anxious, and clawing at the walls. But I was not.

I was...steady.

I still talked to friends in the business. I would hear the stress in their voices, the panic about month-end numbers, the frustration over inventory, the fear of a bad audit. I remembered that feeling. I remembered the chest pains over missing a bonus. I remembered the sleepless nights because a deal fell through.

But now, listening to them, I felt a profound shift. Their emergencies did not feel like emergencies to me anymore.

I found myself being the one to talk them off the ledge. I would listen to them vent, spinning out of control about targets and quotas, and I would simply tell them to breathe.

"It's going to be okay," I would say. "You're going to go home to your family tonight. You are going to eat dinner. You are going to wake up tomorrow. It is just cars. It's not life."

I realized that I was not just comforting them; I was comforting the old version of myself. I was speaking the truth I wish someone had spoken to me twenty years ago.

I learned that the world does not fall apart just because I stop holding it up.

That was the fruit of surrender. It gave me a perspective that insulated me from the petty tyrannies of urgent but unimportant things.

🍎🍎🍎

But surrender is not a magic shield against fear. The fear still tries to come back, especially in the dark.

In the book of Daniel, there is a story about three young men— Shadrach, Meshach, and Abednego. They are threatened with a fiery furnace if they do not bow down to a false king. Their response is the greatest definition of faith I have ever read.

They say to the king: *"Our God whom we serve can deliver us from the burning fiery furnace…But if not, be it known to you, O king, that we will not serve your gods."*

But if not. Or in some translations, *Even if He does not.*

For a long time, my faith was conditional. It was transactional. It was the faith of a dealmaker.

God, if You heal me, I will trust You. God, if You fix this business deal, I will praise You. God, if You keep my family safe, I will follow You.

That is not faith. That is a negotiation. That is a contract. And God does not sign contracts written by men.

Real faith says: *God, I believe You can heal me. You have the power to wipe this cancer from my body in a microsecond. But even if You do not, You are still good, and I will still trust You.*

That shift is terrifying. It requires letting go of the outcome completely. It requires accepting that God's goodness is not defined by my physical comfort or even my survival.

When I finally got to the place where I could say, "Lord, I want to live. But even if my story ends sooner than I want, I know I am safe with You." At that point, the fear lost its teeth.

It could not threaten me anymore because the worst-case scenario—death—was no longer a defeat. It was just a different kind of healing. It was a promotion.

Of course, theology is great until you are facing a CT scan.

"Scanxiety" is real. Every three months, I had to go back into the tube to see if the monster was sleeping or waking up.

The days leading up to a scan were a mental war. Every ache was analyzed. *Is that back pain a tumor growing? Is that cough a metastasis or just allergies?* My mind would start to race, writing chapters of a tragedy that had not happened yet.

And then there is the waiting. The days between the scan and the results are the longest days of your life. You walk around with a knot in your stomach. You look at your phone every time it buzzes, wondering if it is the doctor.

In the past, I would have spiraled. I would have let the fear consume me until I was paralyzed.

But this time, I had to practice what I preached. I had to use the surrender I had found under the oak tree.

I realized that I was suffering in advance. I was paying interest on a debt I might never owe. I was letting my imagination draft the report before the doctor did.

That experience taught me to guard my mind aggressively. The Bible says to "take every thought captive." I realized that was not a suggestion; it was a command for mental survival.

I started treating my thoughts like visitors at the front door of my house. When a thought knocked—*You are not going to make it, the cancer is spreading*—I checked its ID.

Is this true? I do not know yet. *Is this helpful?* No. *Does this come from God?* No.

Then you cannot come in.

I had to slam the door on those thoughts. Sometimes I had to slam the door a hundred times a day. I had to forcibly redirect my mind from "What if" to "What is."

What is true right now? I am breathing. I am here. God is faithful.

Two days later, the results would come back. Stable. No change. Or shrinkage.

The worry had been for nothing. The fear had been a liar. My lack of surrender had not changed the scan results; it had only stolen my peace for three days.

Surrender did not cure my cancer. The medicine and God's grace did that.

But surrender cured my soul.

It cured me of the exhaustion of trying to be god of my own life. It taught me that the view from the passenger seat is beautiful, if you trust the Driver.

I still have days when I try to grab the wheel. It is human nature. I start planning, worrying, and projecting. I start feeling that old tightness in my chest, the "fixer" trying to wake up.

But now, I know the cure.

I sit down—mentally or physically—and I open my hands.

And I say the prayer that saved me, not from death, but from despair:

I cannot fix this. But You can. And even if You do not fix it the way I want, I trust You.

That is the taste of turnip greens. It is bitter going down. It requires chewing. It requires swallowing your pride. But once it is in you, it builds a strength that sugar never could.

I was no longer fighting against the current. I was learning to float. And the water, I discovered, was full of grace.

CHAPTER 10

Turnip Greens & the Lens of Gratitude
Part 1: The "I Get To" Revolution

When I was a boy growing up in Georgia, the dinner table was often a courtroom, and I was the defendant on trial. The evidence against me? A steaming pile of dark, leafy greens sitting in the center of my plate like a wet accusation.

Turnip greens.

If you are not from the South, you might not understand the complexity of turnip greens. They are not like spinach, which wilts politely. They are not like lettuce, which is crisp and refreshing. Turnip greens are tough. They are fibrous. They taste like the earth they were pulled from—bitter, mineral-heavy, and pungent.

I hated them. I would push them around my plate with my fork, building little dams of cornbread to hold back the *"potlikker"* juice, hoping that if I moved them enough, my parents might think I had eaten some.

Mom would stand over me, a dish towel thrown over her shoulder, and say the same thing every time.

"Eat your greens, Jerry. They'll make you strong."

I did not want to be strong. I wanted to be happy. And in my ten-year-old mind, happiness tasted like macaroni and cheese, not boiled leaves.

But the rule was simple: You eat the bitter to get to the sweet. You swallow the rough stuff because it builds something inside you that sugar never will.

It took me forty years, a career burnout, and a Stage 4 cancer diagnosis to finally understand what Mom was talking about.

Life serves us all a bowl of Turnip Greens eventually. It serves us heartbreak. It serves us failure. It serves us sickness. And our first instinct is always the same: push the plate away. We want the blessing without the burden. We want the testimony without the test. We want resurrection without the cross.

But during the long months of treatment—when the metal taste was in my mouth and the fatigue was in my bones—I learned that if you push away the bitter parts of life, you starve. You miss the nutrition that God has hidden inside the struggle.

Gratitude became my fork. It was the tool I used to digest the hard things without letting them make me bitter.

🌱🌱🌱

Gratitude is easy when the sun is shining.

When the bonus check clears, when the scan comes back clean, when the kids are behaving, when the Georgia Bulldogs win—it is easy to look up and say, "Thank You, God." That is reactive gratitude. It is a response to good circumstances. It costs you nothing.

But proactive gratitude? That is discipline. That is a weapon.

Proactive gratitude is looking at a storm cloud and thanking God for the rain before a single drop hits the ground. It is sitting in a chemotherapy chair, feeling the poison enter your veins, and thanking God that there is medicine available to fight for your life.

It sounds noble in theory. In practice, it is a dogfight.

I remember a specific Tuesday. It was a "low" day. The treatment was doing a number on me. My energy was gone. My skin was breaking out in a rash from the medication. I felt heavy, like I was wearing a lead vest.

I dragged myself out of bed and shuffled to the kitchen. I wanted one thing: Coffee. I needed the ritual. I needed warmth to wake up my system.

I stood at the counter while the machine brewed, gripping the granite edge just to hold myself up. My legs ached. My head pounded. And in the quiet of that morning, self-pity started to rise like bile.

Why is this so hard? I thought. *I am fighting for my life. I cannot walk without pain. I am tired of being tired.*

It was not that anything specific had gone wrong that morning; it was just the accumulation of it all. The weight of the diagnosis felt unbearable. I felt abandoned by the universe, stuck in a body that was betraying me.

Then, I looked up.

I caught a glimpse of the backyard through the kitchen window. The sun was just cresting over the pine trees, painting the sky in bruised purples and fiery oranges. It was a masterpiece. It was a show that God put on every single morning, usually while I was too busy complaining or rushing to notice.

I took a breath. I remembered the oak tree. I remembered the surrender.

Do not spiral, I told myself. *Shift the lens.*

"Thank You for the sunrise," I whispered. It felt forced. I did not feel thankful. I felt sick and grumpy.

I tried again. "Thank You that I have eyes to see it."

A little better.

"Thank You that I have legs to stand here and look at it, even if they hurt."

Better still.

"Thank You that I have a kitchen to stand in. Thank You that I have a home."

By the time I got to "Thank You for the wife sleeping in the other room," the heaviness in my chest had lifted just enough to let the light in.

The situation had not changed—I still had cancer; I still had a rash—but *I* had changed.

That morning taught me that gratitude is a lens. You cannot always change the scenery of your life—sometimes the scenery is a hospital room, or a difficult morning, or a bank account that is too low—but you can change the lens you look through.

If you look through the **Lens of Lack**, you will always see what is missing. You will see the pain, the debt, the unfairness. You will see the Turnip Greens and taste only the dirt.

If you look through the **Lens of Gratitude**, you will see what is present. You will see the provision, the protection, the grace. You will see the minerals in the greens that are making you strong.

Same life. Different lens. The choice is yours.

I started playing a mental game with myself called **"I Get To."**

For years, my vocabulary was built around "I have to." It is the language of the victim. It is the language of burden.

I must go to work. I have to mow the lawn. I must pay the bills. I must go to the doctor.

"Have to" implies that you are a prisoner of your own life. It implies that these things are punishments.

I decided to swap it for "I get to."

On the days I felt well enough to drive myself to the grocery store, I stopped groaning about the traffic on Highway 41. Instead, I gripped the steering wheel and thought, *I get to drive. I get to be independent today. I get to buy food for my family.*

When the lawn needed mowing and the Georgia heat was stifling—95 degrees and sticky—I stopped complaining about the sweat. I thought, *I get to mow this grass. I have a home with a yard. I have lungs that can handle the humidity. I have the strength to push this mower.*

Two months ago, I could not walk to the mailbox. Today, I am mowing the lawn. That is not a chore; it is a victory lap.

It sounds like a small linguistic trick, a mind game. But words have power. Words shape reality. When you change your words, you rewire your brain.

One afternoon, I was sitting in the waiting room for a blood draw. The room was packed. A man across from me was on his cell phone, complaining loudly to whoever was on the other end. He was angry about the wait time. He was angry about parking. He was angry about the reception he got on his phone.

"It's ridiculous," he snapped. "I have to be here every week. It's a waste of my time."

I listened to him, and I realized: *That used to be me.*

I used to be the guy checking his watch, tapping his foot, furious that the world was not moving on my schedule. I used to be the guy who thought his time was more valuable than everyone else's.

But sitting there that day, feeling the port in my chest, I felt a strange sense of peace. I looked around the room. I saw a young mother with a toddler who was bald from chemo. I saw an elderly couple holding hands, the wife reading to the husband. I saw the receptionist patiently answering the same question for the tenth time.

I get to be here, I thought. *I get to fight for more time. I get to live in an era where medicine exists that can extend my life.*

The angry man hung up his phone and sighed, looking miserable. He was healthy enough to yell, but sick in his spirit. I was sick in my body, but for the first time in years, my spirit felt healthy.

He was starving in front of a banquet because he refused to pick up his fork.

Gratitude turns what we have into enough. It turns a meal into a feast, a house into a home, and a stranger into a friend.

But gratitude isn't something you do once and check off a list. If you keep it inside, or save it only for the good days, it withers. It must be discipline.

Steph and I realized that if we were going to survive the mental toll of cancer, we needed a new operating system. We couldn't wait for things to get better to be thankful; we had to be thankful *so that* we could get better.

We started what I call a **"Gratitude Audit."**

It wasn't a formal meeting or a checklist we kept on the nightstand. It was a movement within our own hearts. It was a conscious decision to shift our focus from what was being taken away to what was still there.

On the good days, the audit was easy. The scan was clear. The steak dinner was great. The boys were happy. Those blessings were low-hanging fruit.

But on the "Turnip Green days"—the days that were bitter, tough, and hard to swallow—we had to dig. We had to mine for the gold in the mud.

There were nights I would lie in bed, exhausted from the side effects, my body feeling heavy and foreign. I wanted to be angry. I wanted to wallow in the unfairness of it all. It would have been easy to list ten things that went wrong that day.

But instead, I forced my mind to scan for the wins.

Sometimes the win was simply that the nausea settled down for an hour so I could eat dinner. Sometimes, it was because it rained, so the pollen count was down, and I could breathe a little easier. Sometimes, the only win I could find was the most important one: **We survived.** The sun went down, and I was still here to see it set.

We didn't always say it aloud, but we lived it. We stopped measuring our days by how much pain I was in and started measuring them by how much grace we could find.

This habit did something powerful: it trained my brain to scan the day for gold.

It works just like buying a new car. You never notice how many white Toyota Camrys are on the road until you buy one, and suddenly, you see them everywhere. Your brain finds what it is looking for.

When you start looking for pain, you will always find it. But when you start looking for grace—for the small mercies, the quiet moments, the survival—you start seeing it everywhere.

You stop letting the pain be the headline of your day. The pain becomes the footnote. Gratitude becomes the story.

Part 2: The Nutrition in the Dirt

This new lens—this determination to find the gold in the mud—did not just change how I viewed my cancer. It changed how I viewed my history.

They say hindsight is 20/20. That is true. Looking back, everything is clearer. But gratitude does something more than clarify; it magnifies. It makes hindsight 40/40. It allows you to see things you completely missed the first time around because you were too busy looking for what you wanted instead of what you needed.

I started looking back at my career in the car business through this new lens. For years, I had viewed those decades with a mixture of pride and regret. I was proud of the numbers, but I regretted the time. I felt guilty for the missed ball games, the late dinners, the stress I brought home to Steph. I looked at the burnout as a failure of my endurance.

But through the lens of gratitude, the picture shifted.

I saw those grueling years not as lost time, but as boot camp. Those bell-to-bell shifts built a resilience in me that I was now using to survive chemotherapy. The ability to handle high-pressure negotiations taught me how to advocate for myself with insurance companies. The thick skin I developed dealing with angry customers helped me handle the indignity of being a patient.

I looked back at the job losses—the times I was demoted or passed over. At the time, I had called them failures. I had called them injustices.

Now, I called them **protections**.

I thought about the "Passover"—the time I lost the GSM job to Ashton. Gratitude allowed me to look at that closed door and say, *"Thank You."*

If I had not been demoted from that job, I would not be where I was now. If I had not taken a chance on a new job, I would not have moved to the new territory with Prestige. I would not be living ten minutes away from Steph's family.

Why does that matter?

Because five years later, when I was lying in a hospital bed unable to walk, we needed that family. We needed Steph's mom to help with the boys.

God had closed a door in 2005 to ensure I had a support system in 2020. He was playing the long game. I was playing checkers; He was playing 3D chess.

Gratitude allowed me to forgive my own history. It allowed me to stop looking at the jagged line of my career and wishing it were straight. It allowed me to say, "God, You were there in the mess, even when I didn't see You. You were plotting my safety when I thought You were ignoring my ambition."

There is a profound freedom in realizing that nothing in your life has been wasted. God uses every scrap of it. The good, the bad, and the bitter. He is the ultimate recycler. He takes the trash of our lives, the mistakes, the pain, the delays—and He composts it into fertilizer for our future.

The ultimate test of this perspective was not a specific event; it was a quiet realization that settled over me during the long months of recovery.

I realized that I would not trade the man I was becoming for the man I used to be—even if it meant getting my kidney back. Even if it meant erasing the Stage 4 diagnosis.

The "Old Jerry" was successful, but he was shallow. He was driven, but he was deaf to the things that really mattered. He measured his worth in receipts and recognition. He was building a kingdom of sand that could be washed away by a single bad month or a single doctor's appointment.

The "New Jerry" was broken, yes. He was sick, yes. He walked with a limp and tired easily. But the light was getting in through the cracks. He was building on the Rock.

I started to thank God for the breaking.

It is a dangerous prayer, but a necessary one.

Thank You for the bitter taste of this season, I would pray, *because it has stripped away my pride.* I used to be arrogant; now I am dependent. And I like the dependent Jerry better.

Thank You for the weakness because it has forced me to lean on Your strength. I used to think I held the world up; now I know You hold me up.

Thank You for the uncertainty because it has taught me to trust. I used to trust my bank account and my five-year plan; now I trust my Savior.

That is the miracle of gratitude. It does not just help you endure the fire; it helps you see the Fourth Man standing in the fire with you. It shifts your focus from the heat of the flames to the hand that is holding you.

So, back to the Turnip Greens.

My mother was right. They tasted like dirt because they came from the dirt. They were full of iron, calcium, and vitamins—nutrients that you cannot get from sweet things.

You cannot get strong on candy. You cannot build muscle on marshmallows. You need iron. And the iron comes wrapped in bitterness.

I finally understood the metaphor of my life.

The car business was a bowl of greens. It was tough. It was gritty. But it gave me the iron of **Resilience**.

The burnout was a bowl of greens. It was exhausting. It was lonely. But it gave me the iron of **Perspective**.

The cancer is the biggest bowl of greens I have ever been served. It is bitter. It is hard to swallow. There are days I choke on it.

But it is giving me the iron of **Faith**.

It is building a spiritual immune system that fear cannot penetrate. It is strengthening my soul in ways that comfort never could.

If you are walking through a dark season right now, if life has served you a plate of something you did not order and do not want—I challenge you to pick up your fork.

Change your lens.

You do not have to be thankful *for* cancer, or divorce, or bankruptcy. God does not expect you to call evil "good." He does not expect you to enjoy the taste of the dirt.

But you can be thankful *in* it.

You can be thankful that you are not walking through the fire alone.

You can be thankful for the strength that is being forged in the heat.

You can be thankful that your story is not over.

Gratitude is the mechanism that turns a victim into a victor. A victim looks at the wreckage and asks, "Why did this happen to me?" A victor looks at the wreckage and says, "I will build something new out of this."

Eat the greens. Swallow the bitter. Trust that the Nutritionist knows what He is doing.

Because one day, you will look in the mirror—scarred, limping, gray—and you will see a strength looking back at you that you never possessed before.

You will realize that the very thing you tried to push off your plate was the thing that saved your life.

And then, just like Mom used to do, God will bring out the Grace. The sweetness that follows obedience. The peace that follows the surrender.

Turnip Greens first. Grace second.

That is the meal. And today, I am cleaning my plate.

Part 3: The Empty Chair

There is a darker side to the Lens of Gratitude. It is not about being thankful for coffee or sunrises. Sometimes, gratitude is the only thing keeping you tethered to the earth when the darkness tries to tell you that leaving would be easier.

I learned this lesson through one of the deepest losses in my life.

Years before my diagnosis—back in May of 2016—we lost my brother-in-law, Ray.

Ray was my sister Terri's husband, but to me, he was a brother. He had entered my life when I was a teenager, at a time when I was trying to figure out who I was. He never treated me like a kid; he treated me like a man in the making. I would follow him around like a puppy at times and I can imagine the moments where he and Terri simply wanted spaced. Especially from Terri's teenage kid brother. He was the one who inspired me to get into the car business. He was the one who showed me that you could build a life with your own hustle.

After years of the car business and seeing the real value in family and time with his children, Ray left car sales and built a successful career as a civil servant. On the surface, things looked stable. But inside, a storm was raging that none of us fully understood.

Ray died by suicide.

To this day, that word hangs in the air, heavy and unresolved.

Suicide is the tragic result of a terrible illness called depression. It is not a weakness of character; it is a sickness of the mind. It is a fog so thick that it blinds you to the things you are passionate about. It convinces you that the burden you carry is too heavy to share, and that the world would be lighter without you in it.

When I was diagnosed with Stage 4 cancer, when I was fighting with every ounce of my strength just to stay on this side of the dirt, I found myself talking to Ray.

I would sit in the infusion chair, watching the medicine drip, and I would think about him. *I wish you were here, Ray.*

I knew, with a certainty that ached in my bones, that if Ray had been around to see my fight, it might have changed his.

If he could have sat with me in that room, looking at the people who were losing their hair, their strength, and their futures, but who were still smiling, still praying, still fighting for *one more day*...I believe he would have seen what he could not see through the fog of his depression.

He would have seen how desperately humans want to live. He would have seen that life, even when it is painful, even when it is limited, is a treasure worth hoarding.

I have often wondered if we should not all spend time serving people who are dealing with a life crisis like cancer. That may be the cure for the apathy that sometimes settles over us. When you sit next to someone who is fighting for breath, you realize what a miracle it is that you can breathe without thinking.

Ray's loss was devastating to me and to our whole family. We still miss him. But his passing taught me a lesson that became a pillar of my own survival: **Every moment matters.** Every conversation is an opportunity to throw a lifeline.

I hope he is looking down on us now. I hope the fog has cleared for him. And I hope he is cheering for me as I make my journey through this life, reminding me to never, ever take the gift of a heartbeat for granted.

CHAPTER 11

The Limp: Second Chances
Part 1: The Bell and the Shadow

There is a tradition in cancer centers across America. A small brass bell, usually mounted on a wooden plaque near the exit. It looks insignificant - like something you might find on a ship or a front porch - but in that building, it is the holiest object in the room.

When you finish your last treatment - when the protocol is complete, the veins have taken all they can take, and the doctor says the words "No Evidence of Disease" - you get to ring it.

It is supposed to be a moment of pure, unadulterated joy. The nurses gather around. Other patients look up from their chairs; their eyes filled with a mix of happiness for you and longing for themselves. You grab the braided cord, give it a sharp tug, and the sound rings out - clean, bright, and final. Ding-ding-ding.

It signals the end of the war.

My day came on May 27, 2022.

It had been two and a half years. Thirty months.

Thirty months of infusions that left a metallic taste in my mouth. Thirty months of thyroid crashes that left me shivering or sweating. Thirty months of scans, pills, fears, and prayers. Thirty months of walking through the valley of the shadow of death.

I stood in front of that bell. Steph was beside me, holding her phone to capture the moment, her hand trembling just slightly. I looked at the cord. My arm shook as I reached for it - not from weakness this time, but from the sheer, crushing weight of the moment.

I pulled it. I pulled it hard.

The sound filled the room, sharp and clear. It cut through the hum of the machines and the quiet murmur of the clinic. The nurses clapped and cheered. Steph, overcome with both joy and relief, wiped a tear.

I hugged them. Then I turned and buried my face in Steph's shoulder. I felt two and a half years of tension leaving my body. The sob came from the deepest part of my soul. It was victory. It was over.

But as we walked out of the infusion center for the last time, stepping into the blinding brightness of May sunlight, a different feeling settled over me. It was not just joy. It was not just relief. It was a heavy, suffocating blanket of guilt.

I looked back at the glass doors. I thought about the people still inside. I thought about the man in the corner with the quilt who never woke up during treatments. I thought about Bill, the guy with the ginger snaps who gave me advice on my first day back in 2020. I had not seen Bill in over a year. I did not know if he had finished his treatment, or if his treatment had finished him.

Why me?

The question nagged at me, relentless and cruel. Why did my body respond to the trial when others did not? Why did the tumors in my lungs shrink while others grew? Why did I get to walk out to my car and drive home to my boys after two and a half years, while someone else was inside hearing that they had three months to live?

I had not prayed harder than them. I was not a better person than them. I was not more deserving. I realized that returning to the world of the living is harder than it sounds. You survive the storm, but you do not know how to live in the calm, because the silence is filled with the ghosts of those who did not make it.

Part 2: The Suit and the Haze

That guilt, mixed with a profound sense of vulnerability, followed me into my closet as I prepared to return to the road.

Since my role with Prestige was remote, "going back to work" did not mean a daily commute. It meant logging on from my home office. But it also meant traveling again - airports, hotels, and standing in front of teams.

I stood there looking at my suits. They were the armor of my previous life. I picked out a navy blue one - my "closer" suit. I put on a white shirt. I tied the tie. I looked in the mirror. The man staring back at me looked like Jerry, but he did not feel like Jerry.

The suit fit a little differently. The battle with my thyroid and the weight fluctuations had changed my shape. But the biggest difference was not visible. It was cognitive.

The old Jerry was sharp. I was a steel trap. I could remember numbers, policies, and procedures without looking them up. I could quote the handbook. I was fast.

The new Jerry was foggy. Treatment had left a haze over my mind. I would be in the middle of a thought and it would evaporate. I would reach for a word and it would not be there. I would read a policy and, five minutes later, I could not recall the details.

I grabbed my suitcase. I drove to the airport. And for the first time in my thirty-year career, I felt like an impostor. Do I still have it? Can I still run with the big dogs? Or am I just a broken guy playing dress-up?

In the corporate finance world, vulnerability is usually seen as blood in the water. It is a high-performance culture. If you show weakness, you get replaced. If you slow down, you get run over. And there I was, walking back into the arena - not as the invincible General Manager, but as a survivor who needed a nap at 2:00 p.m. and had to write everything down just to remember it.

I walked into my first big meeting. The room was full of energy. KPIs (Key Performance Indicators) were on the screen. Territory visits. Growth charts. The old me would have jumped right in. I would have drilled down on the numbers. I would have been the hammer.

But I looked at the faces of my team. I saw their stress. I saw the pressure they were carrying. And I decided to tell the truth. I stood up. I did not look at the screen. I looked at them.

"I want to be honest with you guys," I said. My voice was steady, but my hands were shaking slightly under the table. "I'm back, but I'm not the same. I'm dealing with some things. The treatment saved my life, but it came with a cost. I have brain fog. My memory is not what it used to be. I might forget a policy number. I might need you to remind me of a detail I used to know by heart."

The room went quiet. Leaders do not usually admit to brain fog.

"But here's what else has changed," I said. "I realized that none of this" - I pointed to the KPI charts on the screen - "matters if we are not taking care of ourselves. I spent three years fighting for my life, and it taught me that life is too short to be miserable at work."

I took a breath. "So, we're going to change the focus. Yes, we have a job to do. Yes, we need to hit our numbers. But from now on, our priority is you - your wellness, your families, your mental health. Because if you aren't okay, the numbers don't matter."

I stood there in silence, feeling the weight of the limp, I was now showing the world. The fear of being an impostor began to fade, replaced by the realization that I was not there to be the smartest guy in the room anymore. I was there to be the most human leader in the room.

As I looked around that conference room and saw the relief on their faces, I knew this was a different kind of victory. I was returning with scars, and I was returning with a limp. But for the first time in my life, I wasn't trying to hide it.

CHAPTER 12

Servant Leadership: The Business of People
Part 1: The Keys, the Mentor, and the Shift

In the automotive retail world, there is a piece of paper that rules your life. It is called the "Daily Doc."

It is a spreadsheet that tracks everything: units sold, gross profit, financing penetration, customer satisfaction scores, and expense ratios. For twenty years, I lived and died by that piece of paper. I looked at it before I had my morning coffee. I looked at it before I went to bed. I judged my self-worth - and the worth of my employees - by the totals in the right-hand column.

By the time my cancer treatment came along, I had transitioned into the financial services industry with Prestige, and I had swapped the "Daily Doc" for the DMR (Daily Management Report). Different acronym, same purpose. It was still a scorecard that told me if I was winning or losing based on volume and yield.

But after spending a year in a cancer center, staring at a different kind of report - blood counts, tumor markers, survival probabilities - my relationship with the Daily Doc and the DMR changed forever.

I realized something that should have been obvious, something hidden by ambition and fear of failure:

Spreadsheets do not capture deals. People do.

Spreadsheets do not build relationships.

Spreadsheets do not stay late to help a partner.

Spreadsheets do not care.

This shift was not only about my cancer. It was the culmination of a journey that began decades ago - born from the guilt of how I used to lead and the grace of mentors who showed me a better way.

To understand the leader I became, you must understand the leader I used to be, and the leaders who shaped me - for better and for worse.

I remember a specific Regional Manager from early in my career. Let us call him Richard. Richard ruled by humiliation. He believed shame was the ultimate motivator. He believed that if you made a man feel small enough, he would work hard to feel big again.

Every Monday morning we had a sales meeting. Richard would stand at the front of the room with a big whiteboard and a red marker. He would write everyone's name on the board and their sales figures for the week.

If you had a good week, you were ignored. Excellence was simply the baseline.

If you had a bad week, you were the target.

"Look at this," he would sneer, drawing a big red circle around a low number. "Three cars? My grandmother could sell more cars by accident. Are you even trying? Maybe you should go to work at the shoe store."

Richard thought he was motivating us. He thought he was lighting a fire. But I looked around the room and saw grown men checking out. We did not work harder for Richard; we worked harder to hide from Richard. We stopped taking risks. We stopped helping each other. It created a culture of cannibals.

I hated Richard's style. I vowed I would never be like him.

But the car business is seductive. It rewards aggression. And as a young, overly confident New Car Sales Manager, I fell into the trap. I started to believe you had to be "tough" to make it. If someone was not tough by my standards, I figured it was their fault.

It was too easy to get rid of people. It was easier to fire them than to train them.

I hit my lowest point as a young leader on a Tuesday afternoon. It involved a young employee named David.

One of the other managers had taken David out to lunch. It was a long lunch - too long. And, as fate would have it, David had accidentally taken a set of keys with him. Keys to a car I needed to show a customer right now.

As the minutes ticked by, my frustration boiled over into rage. I was not just worried about the customer; I was worried about my authority. How dare they leave me hanging? Don't they know who I am?

When David finally walked back in, I did not ask for an explanation. I approached him in the middle of the showroom, in front of his peers.

"Where are the keys?" I snapped. "Who said you could take a two-hour lunch?"

I began to interrogate him. I was loud. I was aggressive. I was channeling Richard.

David, flustered, pulled the keys from his pocket, and tossed them onto the desk. They slid across the surface and fell off the edge, clattering onto the floor.

It was an unintentional fumble. But in my angry state, I saw it as an assault. I saw it as disrespect.

I exploded. I overreacted. I told him to get out. I sent him on his way with words meant to cut - words meant to burn bridges.

As he walked out the door, the adrenaline faded, and a cold wave of shame washed over me. I looked around the room. The other salespeople were looking down, pretending to be busy. I realized I had not looked strong; I looked like a bully.

I swallowed my pride - which tasted like bile - and ran out the front door. I followed him into the parking lot.

"David, wait," I said, out of breath. "Come back. I was wrong."

I apologized. I asked him to return.

That moment stayed with me for years. It was a low point. It taught me you cannot lead people if you are busy breaking them.

Thankfully, David forgave me.

David went on to become a successful General Sales Manager, and years later, he joined me at Prestige. To this day, he is one of my best friends and greatest supporters. But I had to earn that friendship back.

That incident planted a seed of regret, but it was not until I left the dealership world and joined Prestige that I saw what true leadership looked like.

That's when I met a man named Bryant. He was the President of the company.

In a corporate world often defined by suits and egos, Bryant was an anomaly. He was kind. He was caring. He did not lead from a distance; he connected.

He knew the names of every one of his 300+ employees. He knew their spouses' names. He knew if their kids played soccer or baseball. He knew which college football team they rooted for. He knew how to get the best out of people not by squeezing them, but by seeing them.

I watched him, fascinated. This was a multi-million-dollar company, and yet it was being led with compassion and sincerity - something I had never seen before.

You were accountable to Bryant, but not because you were threatened. You were accountable because you felt responsible to him. You did not want to let him down because he made you feel like you mattered.

I knew, instantly, that this was the kind of leader I wanted to be.

But change takes time.

When I first started at Prestige, I reported to a VP who had a different style. She was not a "bad" leader, but she managed through insecurity. She tracked whereabouts. She questioned schedules. She created an environment where people felt watched rather than trusted.

The culture was so rigid that stopping for a cup of coffee felt like a dangerous risk. People were terrified to pull into a Starbucks on the way to a client meeting, convinced that a five-minute detour would lead to an interrogation, harassment, or a formal write-up. It was management by surveillance, and it paralyzed them. They were so consumed with the fear of doing the wrong thing that they stopped trying to do the great thing.

As I grew into a VP role myself - and eventually, when that other VP moved on - I saw my chance. I wanted to push back on the culture of surveillance and replace it with the culture of Bryant.

I teamed up with our SVP, and we went to work changing the atmosphere. We put trust, compassion, and empowerment at the forefront.

We stopped drilling people with questions about their schedule.

"I don't care if you stop at Starbucks," I told my team. "I trust you to get the job done. I care about your results, not your receipt."

We shifted the problem-solving dynamic. Instead of solving every problem they brought to me, I started asking, "What do you think we should do?" I wanted their ideas. I wanted them to own the solution.

We changed how we hired. Instead of looking for the "sharks" or forcing people into a mold, we started hiring for character. We looked for high-quality people with integrity.

We realized good people could work anywhere - they have options. We viewed it as a privilege that they chose to work for us, so we wanted them to know they were part of something important.

We led with humility. If a mistake was made, we owned it as a leadership team. We were accountable to our people as much as we expected them to be accountable for their results.

One of the most important tools I used was the 1-on-1 meeting.

I met with each individual employee multiple times a year - not to grill them on numbers, but to listen.

"What is important to you?" I would ask. "What do you want to achieve this year? What do you want to learn?"

And the most critical question: "How can we improve as a leadership team? How can I support you better?"

We learned a lot in those meetings. We learned that simple changes could have massive impacts.

For years, our company conferences required employees to travel on Sundays to be ready for a Monday morning start and fly home late on Friday. It was grueling.

"It cuts into family time," one employee told me. "And traveling in the winter on weekends is a nightmare."

So we changed it. We shortened the conferences. We adjusted the travel days so people could have their weekends back.

The result? Better morale. Higher energy. And, ironically, we got better results from the shorter conference because people were engaged instead of exhausted. We focused on what mattered instead of filling time.

We operated on a simple truth: 90 percent of the work is done by the front line.

My job as a leader was not to do the work; it was to get the best out of that 90 percent. And you get the best out of people by giving them a voice and letting them know they are heard.

Part 2: The Gift and the Mirror

This philosophy of "High Standards, Higher Grace" became the bedrock of my leadership at Prestige. It fundamentally changed how I viewed failure in a corporate environment.

In the high-pressure world of automotive finance, mistakes are rarely cheap. We deal in volume, speed, and risk. A missed stipulation or a wrong calculation can cost the company thousands of dollars in a heartbeat.

In the "Old World" - the world of Richard and the managers who ruled by fear - a mistake was a sign of weakness. It was something that would get you fired. If you cost the company money, you were a liability, and liabilities were cut.

But that approach creates a culture of hiding. When people are terrified of the consequences of failure, they do not stop making mistakes; they just stop admitting them. They stop taking risks. They stop trying to solve problems for the customer because the penalty for guessing wrong is execution.

I decided to take a different approach. I started viewing costly mistakes not as losses, but as tuition.

I remember a specific series of events that tested this new mindset. It involved a Dealer Support Rep we will call Kay.

At Prestige, our business was evolving rapidly. We were changing systems, updating policies, and moving fast to capture market share. Often, technology could not keep up with the changes, which meant our employees had to do a lot of manual workarounds to get deals done.

Kay was a dedicated employee. She was focused on doing the right thing for her dealers, trying to provide the "Prestige Quality Experience" we preached. But in the chaos of manual entry and rapid changes, she made a few mistakes.

They were not small mistakes. They were costly details that slipped through the cracks. And they happened back-to-back.

In most finance companies, there are three strikes and you are out. The old Jerry would have looked at the cost of those errors and made a snap judgment: She is not paying attention. She is costing us money. We need to cut her loose.

But the new Jerry - the one who understood that systems fail and humans are fallible - saw it differently.

We called Kay in for a meeting. She came in looking defeated. She knew she had messed up. She expected the hammer to drop. She expected to be walked out of the building.

Instead, we took a different approach.

"Kay," I said, "we know things are moving fast. We know the system is making you do things manually that should be automated. We aren't here to beat you up."

We talked through the errors. We did not focus on the cost; we focused on the cause. We realized her heart was in the right place - she was trying to help the dealer - but her execution had slipped in the rush.

"We aren't going to fire you," I told her. "We're going to help you fix this. We believe in you."

The relief on her face was palpable. It was not just relief; it was a renewal of commitment.

She did not take that grace for granted. She turned her work around completely. She tightened her process and moved past the issue quickly. She became one of our most reliable reps.

If we had gone on the attack - if we had fired her - we would have lost a good employee, damaged the morale of her team, and still been out the money. Instead, we paid the tuition, and in return we kept a loyal, high-performing employee who knew we had her back.

That is the ROI of grace.

Return on investment is not always about money. Sometimes it is about loyalty. You can buy a person's time with a paycheck, but you can only earn their full discretionary effort - their passion, creativity, and protection - through trust and grace.

🍒🍒🍒

As I have grown older, I have realized the importance of highlighting the success of others over myself.

This is a difficult concept to understand, and even harder to execute. It goes against human nature. We are wired to want the credit. We want applause.

I see this struggle especially in young leaders who remind me of myself twenty years ago. They are chasing titles. They are chasing promotions. They want to know, "What do I have to do to get to the next level?"

They think the answer is to do more, achieve more, and shine brighter. But I must sit them down and tell them the hard truth:

"Your job isn't to be the star anymore. Your job is to build the stage for someone else."

That is a hard pill to swallow when you are twenty-five and ambitious. It feels counterintuitive.

In the cutthroat world of business, we are often taught that you must eat or be eaten. When you lead with service, it is easy for others to view that as weakness instead of kindness.

I have had to remind young leaders time and time again: kindness is not weakness. It takes more strength to be kind when things are going wrong than it does to fly off the handle. Anger is easy. Patience is heavy lifting.

It is hard to make leaders understand that as they build others up, they will earn recognition naturally. It will not be the sugar rush of a quick promotion; it will be the sustainable nutrition of a legacy.

My favorite phrase to my leadership team has become:

"The most amazing gift you can give another person is the ability to do amazing things themselves."

That is the job. It is not to be the hero who saves the day. It is to be the guide who teaches them how to save the day.

This means taking a sincere interest in your employees. It means teaching them how to have success instead of telling them all about the success you have had. It means being the kind of person they want to model themselves after, not just the person they have to obey.

I have learned to listen for one specific word when I interview potential leaders: "I."

When a leader uses the word "I" too often, it tells me everything I need to know. It tells me they are the hero of their own movie.

I did this. I achieved that. I hit the number.

True leadership flips the pronouns. When things go right, the word is "You." You did it. You crushed it. Our people deserve the credit for the wins.

But when things go wrong? The word is "We," or even better, "I."

We need to fix this. I did not support you well enough. I need to understand what I can do better.

We are accountable for improving the situation by better understanding what we can do as leaders, just as much as we expect them to be accountable for their results.

Part 3: The P.Q.E. Standard

This philosophy of "High Standards, Higher Grace" was not tested only with my internal team. It was tested most severely in the way we handled our clients.

Later in my tenure at Prestige - after the cancer battle was behind me and I was fully back in the saddle - I was given an opportunity to lead a section of our business traditionally known as "Underwriting."

In most finance companies, Underwriting is the Department of "No." They are the gatekeepers, the ones looking for reasons to reject a deal, the ones who quote policy and hide behind red tape.

I wanted to change that.

We renamed the department Dealer Support.

It was not just a branding exercise; it was a declaration of intent. I told the team, "We aren't here just to evaluate risk. We are here to support the people who send us business. We want to find a way to say 'Yes.'"

The reality of our industry is that dealers have high expectations and short memories. They have dozens of lending options aside from Prestige. If we are difficult, slow, or rigid, they simply move to the next lender on the list. It was on us to make sure we surpassed all others.

We implemented a culture built around an acronym we named P.Q.E. - the Prestige Quality Experience.

This became the north star of how we serviced our dealers. The idea was simple: We wanted to be thorough, looking at every angle of a deal to improve the funding process and ensure higher success rates, but we also wanted to be the easiest relationship they managed.

To make P.Q.E. real, we had to do something scary for a traditional manager: we had to give away our authority. We had to trust our people.

I partnered closely with J.P., a leader who rarely sought credit but deserved more than most. He was compassionate, caring, understanding, and patient - exactly the ingredients we needed to pull this off.

Another large part of the P.Q.E. process was empowerment. Not only did we need to trust our employees; we also needed to empower them.

J.P. and I allowed our employees to make decisions that included financial gestures. If a dealer was frustrated over a fee, or if we had made a mistake that caused a delay, we gave the team the power to fix it. They could waive a fee. They could offer a concession. They could show flexibility that we had never shown historically.

"You don't have to ask us for permission to do the right thing," we told them. "If it costs us a hundred dollars to save a relationship worth ten thousand, make the call."

It did not happen overnight. We had to retrain people. Employees who were used to being micromanaged were terrified to make financial decisions on their own. They were waiting for the hammer to drop.

But we kept reinforcing it: High Standards, Higher Grace.

There were times we did not get it right. There were times a deal went sideways, or a promise was missed. But because of the culture we built, we did not hide from those mistakes. We owned them. We made good on our commitments, even when it hurt the bottom line for that specific transaction.

Slowly, the culture shifted. The Dealer Support team stopped acting like gatekeepers and started acting like partners. They took pride in their ability to solve problems.

P.Q.E. became a bright spot for our company. It became something the team was proud of. They were not just processing paper; they were managing relationships.

❦❦❦

The ultimate test of any culture is what happens when the leader leaves the room.

As the department grew and our responsibilities expanded, we could not be involved in every transaction. We could not approve every waiver on the spot. We had to step back and let the system run.

In a culture of control, this is when things break. Without the boss there to enforce the rules, standards slip.

But that did not happen.

Because we had empowered them, because we had given them the keys to decision-making, they did not need us to hover. They knew the standard. They knew the heart of what we were building.

We would log on to spot-check deals, and we would see notes in the system: Fee waived for dealer satisfaction due to internal delay. Expedited funding to correct error.

We saw the team making the same decisions we would have made, without saying a word. They were not just following a policy; they were protecting the brand.

What happened next may be the most important part of this shift: our one-on-ones changed. Instead of leading conversations around speed of answer or handle time, we started celebrating milestones and new achievements - realizing that all the motivation we had ever given, all the training and begging, had less impact than the trust and empowerment we gave.

This is when I realized servant leadership is the only leadership that scales.

If you lead by control, your organization can only grow as big as your own capacity. You become a bottleneck.

But if you lead by empowerment - if you build a culture where the values live in the people and not just in the policies - the organization can grow without you. It can thrive even when you are not watching.

It was not just that we funded more deals. It was that we built a team of leaders who did not need a title to do the right thing.

So, to anyone leading a team, running a business, or just trying to make a living:

Look up from the spreadsheet. Put down the phone. Trust your people with the power to do good. Make "doing the right thing" your only non-negotiable.

Because in the end, you are not just building a company. You are building a community. And when the storm comes - and it always comes - that community is the only thing that will keep the ship afloat.

CHAPTER 13

Trust over Talent

Part 1: The Broken Equation

For the first half of my life, I worshiped at the altar of talent.

In both the sales world and the corporate finance world, talent is the golden ticket. We all knew the people who had "it." They walked into a boardroom and the atmosphere shifted. They could command a meeting with pure confidence. They did not need notes. They operated on instinct, memory, and charisma. They were the rainmakers.

I was not always the most naturally talented person in the room - I had to work for my wins - but I believed in the formula. I treated life like a math equation:

Effort + Talent = Success.

It was simple. It was reliable. If I was failing, it meant I needed to add more effort or sharpen my skills. I believed that if I worked harder, studied longer, and pushed further, I could muscle my way through anything. I was the architect of my own destiny, and my skill set was the blueprint.

It is a seductive way to live. It feels empowering. I am the captain of my soul.

But there is a fatal flaw in that theology: it only works if you are whole.

When cancer entered my life - and when treatment began to take its toll on my body and mind - that equation broke.

By early 2021, I was fully immersed in my role at Prestige, but the world around me had changed. COVID-19 had shut everything down. Offices were closed. Car lots were empty. Leadership now happened through screens and phone calls instead of conference rooms and handshakes.

I tried to lean back on my old instincts. I tried to be the old Jerry.

I remember a specific All-Staff call during a difficult month. We were tracking behind on our objectives. The market was volatile. The team was tired and discouraged. In the past, this was where I thrived. This was my moment.

I adjusted the lighting to hide the fatigue in my face. I squared my shoulders and tried to summon the old fire.

"We are not going to lose," I told them. "We are going to grind. We are going to find a way. No excuses."

I used the same phrases that had worked for me years before. The same intensity. The same tone.

When the call ended, I leaned back in my chair, exhausted. My heart was racing. My hands were shaking. I waited for the energy to shift. I waited for momentum.

It never came.

The numbers did not move. The team did not feel inspired; they felt disconnected. They saw a leader trying to sprint while carrying a weight he refused to acknowledge.

What I was offering them was not leadership - it was performance.

For a leader, whose currency is confidence and clarity, the cognitive cost of long-term treatment felt like losing my identity. I could not out-think the fog. I could not hustle my way past exhaustion. My talent could no longer save me.

For the first time, effort and talent were not enough.

All I had left was trust.

Part 2: The Kingmaker Strategy

I had to adapt. Not just tactically, but fundamentally.

Prestige was a fast-moving organization. The markets do not pause for personal hardship. I realized that if I tried to maintain my old grip on control - if I tried to be the leader who knew every detail and solved every problem - I would become the bottleneck.

I had a choice: hold onto control and slow everything down, or let go and trust the people around me.

I had three Assistant Vice Presidents reporting to me: Michelle, Emily, and Lauren. They were capable, driven, and deeply invested in their teams. In earlier seasons of my career, I might have micromanaged them to ensure things were done "the right way" - my way.

But I no longer had the capacity for that, and more importantly, I no longer believed in it.

I called them together on a video call and decided to be honest.

"I need you to carry this," I told them. "I can't be in every detail right now. I need you to run your teams. I need you to tell me what I need to know."

It was a vulnerable admission. I was acknowledging that I was not the superhero anymore. I was asking for help in a culture that rarely rewards it.

Instead of hesitation, I saw resolve.

They stepped up. They handled the operational details. They anticipated issues before they reached my desk. They protected the teams and protected me. They allowed me to focus on vision, alignment, and encouragement - the areas where I could still add the most value.

That was when something shifted.

My limitation became their opportunity. Because I could not do everything, they were given space to prove they could.

I stopped trying to be the smartest person in the room and started trying to be the most dependent.

This led to a new philosophy I call the Kingmaker Strategy.

In the corporate world, there are kings and there are kingmakers. Kings want the spotlight. They want credit. They want everyone to know the success of the kingdom rests on their shoulders.

Kingmakers are different.

Kingmakers identify talent, develop it, and then step back. They put the crown on someone else's head and smile from the shadows.

Before cancer, I wanted to be the king.

After cancer, I understood something deeper: Kings eventually fall. But kingmakers leave a legacy.

Part 3: Trust That Endures

Trust is not passive. It is not soft. It is not a lack of standards.

Trust is active leadership.

It means believing that people will rise when they are given responsibility. It means creating an environment where ownership replaces fear. It means understanding that control may feel safe in the short term, but it suffocates growth in the long term.

I learned that trust does not eliminate mistakes - but it changes how people respond to them. When people know they are trusted, they speak up sooner. They take responsibility faster. They protect the culture without being told to.

Talent can win quarters.

Trust builds teams that last.

As I look back now, I see that my career was never meant to be built on how sharp I was, how fast I could think, or how much I could personally carry. Those things fade.

What endures is trust - earned, given, and multiplied through others.

I am grateful that life forced me to learn that lesson the hard way.

Because when talent fails - and eventually it will - trust is what remains.

CHAPTER 14

The Signature of God
Part 1: The Geography of Grace

Every artist signs their work.

Painters scrawl their names in the bottom corner of the canvas in oil. Sculptors chisel their initials into the base of the stone. Authors put their names on the spine of the book. It is a claim of ownership. It says, *"I made this. This belongs to me. This is a finished work."*

For a long time, I looked at the timeline of my life and saw a series of random scribbles. I saw jagged lines of career changes, dark splotches of health crises, and the chaotic shadows of disappointment. It did not look like a masterpiece. It looked like a mess. It looked like a child had taken a crayon to the wall.

But there is a peculiar clarity that comes with distance.

When you stand too close to an Impressionist painting, all you see are chaotic dots of color. It looks like a mistake. It is only when you step back—five feet, ten feet, twenty years—that the dots merge. Chaos resolves. And suddenly, you see the water lily. You see the sunset. You see the face of God looking back at you.

As I stepped back from the intensity of the cancer battle and the grind of my career, I finally stood far enough away to see the picture. And there, hidden in the details, I saw it.

The Signature.

God does not sign His work with ink. He signs it with timing. He signs it with "coincidences" that are mathematically impossible. He signs it with closed doors that save your life and open doors that save your soul.

※ ※ ※

They say hindsight is 20/20. Biblical hindsight is 20/200—it lets you see things that were miles away from your understanding at the time.

I look back now at the "Passover," the job loss that crushed me in my thirties. At the time, I was furious. I felt rejected. I questioned my worth and my skill. I spent months stewing in bitterness, watching Ash, thinking I had been robbed.

But looking back through the lens of the Signature, I see the protection. And I see the positioning.

If I had gotten that promotion, I would have stayed in that dealership. I would have stayed in that town. I would have been locked into a grind that would have kept me geographically anchored to a place where we had no support system.

Getting uncomfortable forced me to pivot. It pushed me toward the financial services industry. It led me to Prestige. And that job required me to move to my new territory.

We moved to Atlanta. We moved ten minutes away from Steph's parents.

At the time, it just seemed like a convenient logistical decision. *Free babysitting*, we thought. *Nice schools*.

But God knew the calendar.

He knew that five years later, I would be lying in a hospital bed unable to walk. He knew Steph would be drowning in the responsibilities of being a caregiver to a Stage 4 cancer patient while trying to raise two boys.

He knew we would need her mom and dad to pick up the kids from school. He knew we would need her dad to fix things around the house when I could not lift a hammer. He knew we would need a village.

If I had won the job I wanted back then, I would have been fighting cancer isolated and alone. We would have broken under the weight.

God closed a door in my thirties to ensure I had a lifeline in my forties.

He was playing the long game. The job loss was not a rejection; it was a relocation. It was the **Geography of Grace**.

I think about the back pain that started this whole journey.

At the time, it was a nuisance. It was an interruption. I complained about it constantly. I blamed the rental cars. I blamed the hotel beds. I tried to medicate it away with ibuprofen and heating pads. I resented it.

But that pain was a messenger.

Renal cell carcinoma is a silent killer. It often has no symptoms until it is too late. It hides deep in the retroperitoneum, growing quietly, expanding until it invades other organs. By the time you feel it in your kidney, you are usually dead.

But I had a bad back. I had arthritis. I had disc compression.

If my back had not hurt, Steph would never have made the chiropractor appointment. If the chiropractor had not failed to fix it, Steph never would have called the orthopedist. If the orthopedist had not ordered the MRI for my *spine*, the radiologist would never have seen the shadow on my *kidney*.

The tumor was an "incidental finding." That is the medical term for stumbling upon a bomb while looking for a lost coin.

That back pain—the thing I cursed, the thing I prayed for God to take away—was the alarm bell that saved my life. It was the smoke detector going off before the house burned down.

It was the Signature of a God who loved me enough to allow me to hurt so that I could heal.

How often have we cursed the very things that were sent to save us? How often have we prayed for God to remove an obstacle, not realizing the obstacle was a barricade keeping us from driving off a cliff?

🍒🍒🍒

There is a concept I call **"Grace in the Gaps."**

There is a spiritual law that works just like gravity: *You reap what you sow.*

In the car business, and later at Prestige, I had spent years trying to sow into people. I tried to treat them fairly. I tried to mentor them. I tried to be generous with my time and my experience. But when you are a leader, you never really know if it is landing. You wonder if people only respect you because you sign the checks or hold the title.

Then, the sickness hit. And the harvest came in.

It was not a financial transaction. It was something far more valuable. It was a professional and emotional safety net that caught me when I fell.

During the darkest months of treatment, there was a massive gap between the job I needed to do and the energy I had to do it. I was a Vice President. I had targets, teams, and responsibilities. But I also had brain fog, fatigue, and appointments that pulled me away from my desk.

The "financial stress" was not about paying bills—Steph managed that. The stress was the fear of losing my relevance. I worried that if I could not perform at 100 percent, the business would suffer, or I would be replaced.

But God had already positioned the answer.

The harvest looked like my AVPs—Michelle, Emily, and Lauren—stepping into the gap without being asked. They did not just do their jobs; they protected mine. They managed issues before they became problems. They managed the culture we had built, ensuring that the team did not slip even when I was not there to enforce it.

It looked like the texts and emails that flooded my phone. Not asking for things but offering them.

"We got this, Jerry. Rest." "We resolved the issue with that GM at the dealership. Don't worry about it." "Just wanted you to know we're praying for you today."

I realized that for years, I thought I was just building a high-performing team. I did not know I was building a fortress that would shelter me in the storm.

That is the Signature of God.

He ensures that no act of mentorship is ever wasted. He stores them up. He keeps the accounts. And when you are in your hour of need, He withdraws the deposit in the form of loyalty, competence, and grace.

I looked at my team—my friends—and I did not just see employees. I saw God's provision wearing headsets and analyzing credit apps. They were the hands that held the business up so I could lay my burden down.

If you ever wonder if doing the right thing matters, if you ever wonder if treating people with kindness pays off, I am living proof that it does.

You are never just doing a job. You are planting seeds. And you have no idea when you might need the shade of the tree you are planting today.

Part 2: The Watchman and the Finished Work

Sometimes, God's signature does not look like a check in the mail or a closed door. Sometimes, it does not look like a doctor's report or a job offer.

Sometimes, it comes on four legs, covered in white fur with black spots, weighing about fifteen pounds.

His name was Benji.

We rescued him from the animal shelter when he was about eighteen months old. He was a Shih Tzu—small, scruffy, and full of a personality that was far too big for his body. We nicknamed him "The Biggest B." It was a title that sounded tough, like a heavyweight boxer or a rapper, but it belonged to a dog that liked to sleep on silk pillows.

From the moment we brought him home, he decided that I was his person. Since I spent my time working from home in those years with Prestige, he became my shadow. If I was in the office on a conference call, Benji was under the desk, warming my feet. If I moved to the kitchen for coffee, Benji's nails clicked on the hardwood right behind me. We were inseparable.

But I did not realize the depth of his purpose until the sickness started.

They say dogs have a sixth sense, an ability to detect shifts in the atmosphere or biology that humans miss. I believe Benji knew I was sick before the doctors did.

In the weeks leading up to my first diagnosis—before the back pain became unbearable—he changed. He became Velcro. He would not leave my side. When I sat down, he would nudge my hand or rest his head on my leg, staring up at me with big, soulful eyes, as if he were trying to tell me, *"I know. I am here. Pay attention."*

Then came the surgery. The partial nephrectomy.

I went into the hospital, fought the battle, and came home to recover. I was weak. I was in pain.

And shortly after I came home, something strange happened. Benji got sick.

He stopped eating. He became lethargic. We rushed him to the animal hospital. The vet ran tests. He came back into the room with a grim look on his face.

"His kidneys are failing," the vet said.

It felt like a cruel irony. It felt like a bad joke. Here I was, recovering from kidney cancer, nursing a kidney that had been sliced in half, and my best friend was fighting a losing battle with his own kidneys.

It was as if he was trying to carry the sickness for me. As if he had absorbed the shock so I would not have to bear it alone.

We treated him. It was touch and go. But just like his owner, "The Biggest B" was a fighter. He turned a corner. The vet was surprised, but pleased. They were able to reverse the failure, and he came back to us, tail wagging, ready to resume his post.

Then came the second diagnosis. Stage 4.

When the cancer returned and spread to my lungs, Benji seemed to understand that the stakes had been raised. He went from being a companion to being a sentry.

During the treatment months, when the fatigue from the clinical trial was crushing and the side effects left me hollowed out, Benji became my constant.

I would come home from the infusion center, exhausted, smelling of antiseptic and fear. I would sink into my recliner, too tired to talk to Steph, too tired to explain to the boys how I felt.

And there was Benji.

He did not ask for a walk. He did not ask for food. He did not ask me to throw a ball. He would simply hop into my lap, curl into a ball against my chest, and sigh. He offered warmth and companionship that demanded nothing in return.

In the middle of the night, when the "what-ifs" woke me up and the anxiety threatened to take over, I would reach down off the side of the bed. He was always there, sleeping on the rug right next to me. I would feel his fur. I would hear his steady breathing in the dark.

And that rhythm would ground me. It was a reminder that I was not alone in the fight. He was standing guard.

Benji walked with me through the valley. He saw me at my weakest. He loved me when I was bald, frail, and frustrated. He loved me when I was angry.

And then, in 2021, the tide turned. The treatments worked. The tumors shrank. I stabilized. I started walking again. I started living again.

A few months after I got the "all clear" to resume a normal life, Benji's kidneys failed again.

This time, he could not fight it. This time, the vet shook his head.

Losing him broke my heart. I cried like a baby. But as I look back through the lens of faith—through the lens of the Signature—I see the timing clearly.

Benji came into my life a few years before the cancer. He stayed through the surgery. He fought back from the brink to stand guard during the chemo. And he only let go once he knew I was going to be okay.

It was as if his assignment was complete.

God sends us specific comforts for specific seasons. He knew I would need a companion who did not need words. He knew I would need a creature whose love was unconditional, unrelated to my performance or my health.

So, He sent Benji.

People might say, "It's just a dog." But I know better.

Benji was a vessel of grace. He was a furry, four-legged signature of God, reminding me that even in the darkest nights, comfort is never far away. He was a security guard who did not leave his post until morning came.

※ ※ ※

There is a story in the Old Testament that sums up my entire theology of suffering. It is the story of Joseph.

Joseph was a young man with big dreams. But his life went off the rails. He was thrown into a pit by his jealous brothers. He was sold into slavery. He was falsely accused of rape. He was thrown in prison for years for a crime he did not commit.

It looked like a wasted life. It looked like a tragedy. It looked like God had abandoned him.

But at the end of the story, through a series of divine "coincidences," Joseph ends up as the second most powerful man in Egypt. He uses his position to save nations from starvation during a famine, including the brothers who betrayed him.

When his brothers stand before him, terrified that he will take revenge, Joseph speaks the words that have become the bedrock of my life.

"You intended to harm me, but God intended it for good to accomplish what is now being done, the saving of many lives."

That is the Signature.

You intended it for harm. The cancer intended to kill me. The stress intended to break me. The fear intended to silence me. The job loss intended to bankrupt me.

But God intended it for good.

He used the cancer to kill my pride. He used the stress to reveal my need for rest. He used fear to teach me faith. He used the job loss to position me for survival.

I am not thankful *for* cancer. I do not call sickness "good." Sickness is a result of a broken world. But I am thankful for *what God did with* the cancer.

I am thankful that He is a Master Artist who can take a black streak of paint—a streak that looks like it ruins the canvas—and turn it into a shadow that gives the whole painting depth and perspective.

Without the shadow, the light does not shine as bright.

If you are in the middle of a messy chapter right now, and you cannot see the Signature, do not panic.

You are too close to the canvas.

You are staring at a dark splotch of pain, and it looks like a mistake. It looks like the Artist slipped. It looks like chaos.

But wait.

Step back. Give it time. Give it faith.

One day, you will turn the page, or you will look back from a higher mountain, and you will see how that dark moment was the necessary contrast for the light that followed.

You will see that the delay was protection. You will see that the rejection was redirection. You will see that the silence was intimacy.

God is authoring a story with your life that is far more complex and beautiful than the one you tried to write for yourself. The story you wanted to write was a straight line: *Success, success, success, retirement.*

God is authoring a story of redemption. And redemption requires something to be redeemed. It requires a struggle.

He has not put the pen down. He has not walked away from the easel.

Trust the Artist.

He signs His work. And when He signs it, it is finished. And it is good.

I look at my life now—the scars, the limp, the gray hair, the slower pace—and I do not see a damaged man. I see a finished work. I see a man who has been chiseled by grace until the image of God started to show through.

And for that, I would go through the fire all over again.

CHAPTER 15

The Rules of the Road

A Manifesto for the High-Performance Soul

Over the last thirty years, from the grocery store to the dealership, from the infusion chair to the executive boardroom, I have collected a set of truths.

Some truths came from mentors like Greg and Bryant. Some from failure and regret. Others came in the quiet moments, sitting alone in a hospital room, listening to machines breathe for me while I wondered what would come next.

These are not slogans. They are not theories. They are guardrails.

When the fog sets in—whether it is chemo brain, exhaustion, fear, or simply the chaos of a busy Tuesday, these are the markers I look for to stay on the road.

If I could sit down with a young leader or leave something behind for my sons to read when life gets heavy, this is what I would give them.

How to Think

Control Your Attitude Relentlessly

You cannot control how smart you are today or how fast you move up tomorrow. You *can* control your attitude in this moment. I have seen talented people fail because they were miserable, and average people rise because they were relentless. Attitude multiplies ability. A bad one divides it.

Be Honest with Yourself

Ignorance is growing a hairstyle that everyone else knows is ugly. We all have blind spots but pretending they do not exist only deepens them. If you are failing, admit it. If you are scared, say it aloud. You cannot fix a problem you refuse to name.

Understand Seasons of Pain

Your hands blister before they callus. Trouble, like a rose, has thorns and demands attention—but it also has a season. Do not quit while you are being toughened. Do not make permanent decisions in temporary pain.

Speak the Language of Gratitude

Stop saying "I have to." It is the language of a prisoner. You *get to* work. You *get to* have responsibility. You *get to* fight for your health. Gratitude does not change your circumstances—it changes how you carry them.

How to Lead

Trust Is Not Soft

Trust is not passive, and it is not weak. It is active leadership. When people know they are trusted, they speak up sooner, take responsibility faster, and protect the culture without being told. Talent can win quarters. Trust builds teams that last.

Build the Stage, Not the Spotlight

The hardest lesson for ambitious leaders is this: your job is no longer to be the star. Your job is to build a stage for someone else. Recognition earned through service lasts longer than applause chased through ego.

Take Good Care

The people in your care deserve your best, just as you expect their best. Leadership is not a one-time investment—it is daily, often inconvenient, and sometimes exhausting. But when you pour into others consistently, you prepare them for success long after you are gone.

Never Stop Learning

The moment you think you know it all is the moment you start shrinking. Some of the greatest lessons I learned came from people who reported to me. Humility keeps leaders alive. Curiosity keeps them relevant.

How to Live

Enjoy the Party

Do not wait for the promotion, the raise, or the clean scan to celebrate. The party is life itself—the time, the people, the opportunity in front of you. If you only celebrate outcomes, you miss the joy of the journey.

Character Over Cash

No amount of money is worth the cost of your integrity. You can earn money back. You cannot recover a lost name. I have seen men trade character for commissions and lose everything that mattered in the process.

Make a Difference Every Day

You do not have to save the world. Just make the person standing next to you feel a little better than they did before they met you. If you do that consistently, your life will compound in quiet, meaningful ways.

Eat the Greens

Do the hard thing. Have the uncomfortable conversation. Take the medicine. Apologize first. Forgive when you do not want to. The bitter things are usually the ones that make you strong. If you push the plate away, you stay weak. If you eat the greens, you grow.

These are the rules I try to live by—not perfectly, but intentionally.

They have carried me through boardrooms and hospital rooms, through wins and losses, through fear and gratitude.

They are not guarantees. They are guides.

And when the road gets dark—as it always does at some point—I trust they will keep me moving forward.

EPILOGUE

The Golf Cart & the Next Chapter

These days, if you want to find me, do not look for me in the conference room. Do not look for me at the airport. Do not look for me in the glass office.

Look for the golf cart.

We live in a community where it is common to see neighbors cruising around in the evenings on electric carts. It is a simple machine. It tops out at about fifteen miles per hour. It does not have climate control. It does not have Bluetooth surround sound. It is not impressive by any metric of the "Old Jerry."

But it has become my sanctuary.

In the evenings, when the Georgia heat finally breaks and the sun starts to dip low behind the pine trees, painting the sky in streaks of violet and gold, Steph and I climb into that cart. Sometimes the boys—who are growing into men before my eyes—squeeze onto the back.

We drive. Nowhere in particular. Just a loop.

Before the cancer, I would have hated the golf cart. I would have despised the speed. *Fifteen miles per hour?* I would have thought. *We are wasting time. We could be getting there faster.* My internal speedometer was always set to eighty. I was always leaning forward, trying to get to the next destination, the next deal, the next achievement.

But now, I love the speed.

Fifteen miles per hour is the speed of observation.

At fifteen miles per hour, you can see the neighbors waving from their porches, and you have time to wave back. At fifteen miles per hour, you can feel the temperature drop ten degrees when you drive through a patch of shade under the oaks. At fifteen miles per hour, you can hear your wife tell you about her day without the roar of the highway or the distraction of the radio drowning her out.

The golf cart taught me that life is not about how fast you can get to the destination. It is about who is sitting next to you on the ride.

As I write this, it is 2025.

The world has changed since I first walked into the Doctor's office. The pandemic is history. The masks are gone. My slightly thinning hair has grown back, though it is a little thicker and grayer now. The scars on my abdomen have faded to silvery lines, maps of a territory I once conquered.

But the greatest evidence of that conquest isn't a scar; it's a memory from earlier this year.

It was the 2025 MLB All-Star Game here in Atlanta. I was there with my sons, Bradley and Dawson. We were surrounded by the noise and energy of the crowd, eating hot dogs, laughing, debating stats—doing the very things I was terrified I would never get to do with them again.

Then, in the middle of the game, everything stopped. The players, the umpires, the fans, everyone froze. It was the "Stand Up To Cancer" moment.

Tens of thousands of people stood up, holding placards with names on them. Names of people they loved. Names of people they lost. Names of people fighting.

I stood up. Bradley and Dawson stood up beside me.

As I held my sign, looking around that stadium at the sea of people standing in silence, I felt a surge of pride that nearly knocked me over. I wasn't standing as a victim. I wasn't standing as a patient. I was standing as a father who had fought to be there.

I stood for the ones who couldn't. I stood for Ray. I stood for my sister-in-law. I stood for Bill and the people in the infusion center who never got to ring the bell.

In that moment of silence, flanked by the two young men I love more than life itself, I realized that I wasn't just a survivor of a disease.

I was part of an army of hope. And I knew, right then, that every painful step of the last five years, every needle, every scan, every prayer, was worth it just to be standing on my feet in that stadium.

※ ※ ※

But life, as it always does, brings new servings of Turnip Greens even after the victory.

As I sit here in 2025, the horizon is cloudy. We are facing new challenges—economic uncertainty is rising, the news is full of reports about unemployment and market shifts, and the automotive finance industry is turbulent. And personally, the battle isn't "over" in the sense that I can walk away; the medical scans continue. They are a quarterly rhythm, a persistent reminder of fragility.

There is a sense of impending change in the air. The stability I have enjoyed at work for the last thirteen years feels less certain than it used to. The ground is shifting again.

If this had happened to the "Old Jerry," the Jerry of Chapter 3, or even Chapter 4, I would be panicking right now.

I would be pacing the floors at 3 a.m. I would be calculating my net worth, terrified that I was about to lose everything. I would be angry at the economy. I would be questioning my worth. *I'm too old to navigate a storm like this,* I would think. *What if I lose my footing?*

But the man sitting in the golf cart this evening is not that man anymore. The man who stood in that stadium with his sons is not afraid of the future.

I look at this uncertainty, and I do not feel panic. I feel peace.

Don't get me wrong, uncertainty is bitter. Not knowing what the next year holds for my career or the economy is tough to swallow. It comes with questions. It comes with a change in routine.

But I have learned the lesson of the greens.

I know that this bitterness is not a poison; it is a nutrient.

I know that if God closes a door, it is because He has already prepared the hallway to the next room.

I know that my identity is not "Vice President." My identity is "Survivor." My identity is "Child of God." And nothing can change that.

I look ahead at Steph, sitting next to me, the wind blowing her hair. She isn't worried either. She has seen God part the Red Sea of Stage 4 cancer; she knows He can handle anything that comes our way.

While we may not know what comes next, we know it will be good.

When I was a kid growing up in the South, the dinner table was a courtroom, and I was always on trial. The evidence against me was that steaming pile of dark leaves.

I used to push them around my plate, building dams of cornbread, dreading every bite. They tasted like earth. They tasted hard. They tasted like something you ate because you had to, not because you wanted to.

Mom would stand over me, a towel thrown across her shoulder, and say the same thing every time.

"Eat your greens, Jerry. They're good for you."

I did not believe her then. How could something that tasted so tough be "good"? Good was ice cream. Good was easy.

But Mom knew something I did not. She knew that strength is not built on sugar. It is built on iron. And the only way to get the iron is to eat the greens.

Now, forty years later, sitting on the other side of a life that has seen both the highest summits of success and the deepest valleys of illness, I finally understand.

Life is a lot like that dinner plate.

God serves us things we do not want. Challenges we never asked for. Pain we never expected. Delays we cannot explain. Endings we did not write.

Our instinct is to push them away. We pray for God to take the plate back to the kitchen and bring us something sweeter. We bargain. We complain. We ask, "Why me?"

But God, in His infinite, severe mercy, says, *"Eat. It is good for you."*

He knows that the character we need to survive cannot be built in good times. He knows that faith is like a muscle—it only gets stronger when it pushes against resistance. He knows that if He gave us everything we wanted, we would remain spiritual children—spoiled, weak, and unprepared for eternity.

So, He gives us the Turnip Greens.

He gave me the car business to teach me grit. He gave me the burnout to teach me balance. He gave me cancer to teach me trust. He gave me the end of my career to teach me dependency.

They were bitter going down. There were days I choked on them. But today, I am stronger, wiser, and more alive than I have ever been, because I did not push the plate away.

And then, there is Grace.

Just like Mom used to put a little piece of fatback in the greens to help them go down, God laces our struggles with Grace.

Grace is the wife who never leaves your side. Grace is the peace that wakes you up in the morning. Grace is the quiet assurance that no matter how bitter the leaf, you are never eating alone.

These days, I find myself pausing more often. I look at my scars not with resentment, but with respect. They are the receipts of the price I paid to become who I am.

Every breath feels like a second chance. Every sunrise feels like a promise kept. And every day reminds me that God did not just bring me *to* the valley…He stayed with me *in* it.

So, here is to the lessons. Here's to the scars. Here is to the bitter things that made us better.

I am ready for the next chapter. I do not know the title of it yet. I do not know if the plot twists.

But I know the Author. And He writes good endings.

So, eat the greens. Trust the Chef. And live for today.

Because in the end, that is what a life well lived really tastes like:

Turnip Greens and Grace.

ACKNOWLEDGMENTS

This book may have my name on the spine, but it was written by a village. No one survives a storm alone, and no one builds a life without a foundation laid by others.

To my Lord and Savior: For the breath in my lungs. You are the Author of my story, even the chapters I didn't want to write. Thank You for the grace that caught me when I fell and the strength that stood me back up.

To Stephanie: You are the hero of this book. You are the General, the Gatekeeper, and the Love of my life. Thank you for holding the ropes when I couldn't hold on myself. Thank you for the nights you stayed awake so I could sleep, and for loving me through the sickness and the health. I am the man I am because you loved me.

To Bradley and Dawson: You are my greatest legacy. Thank you for giving me a reason to fight every single day. Watching you grow into young men of character is the joy of my life.

To Mom and Dad: Thank you for the roots and the rules. Thank you for the dinner table lessons and, yes, even the Turnip Greens. You taught me that hard work is holy work, and that integrity is the only currency that matters.

To my sisters and my extended family: Thank you for the prayers and the support. **To Ray:** I miss you every day, brother. I hope this story honors the impact you had on my life.

To my Medical Team: Thank you for asking the hard questions and catching the shadow. Thank you for guiding us through the unknown at the start of the battle, and continuing to guide me today with expertise and compassion. To the nurses in the infusion center who made "The Chair" a place of hope rather than fear. You gave me the gift of time.

To the Mentors who shaped me:

To **Bill**, for giving a sixteen-year-old kid a chance.

To **Greg**, who didn't just teach me to sell; you taught me how to believe in myself when I didn't know how.

To **Mrs. Jessie**, whose wisdom and command to "Be Still" changed the trajectory of my life.

To **Scott**, who saw potential in me when I was just an "Interim" and petitioned for me to have the chance to achieve my dream of becoming a General Manager.

To my Prestige Family:

To **Bryant**, our former CEO, for showing me that a leader can lead with a heart of gold.

To Mitchell: You were more than a leader, supervisor, and boss; you were a friend who stuck by my side. Thank you for believing in me, supporting me, and never giving up on me, even when the road got hard.

To J.P., Ryan, and Sara: Thank you for your partnership and leadership and for making Prestige a better place.

To Michelle, Emily, and Lauren: For carrying the load when I was weak—you are the definition of a dream team.

To Every Employee who sent a text, gave encouragement, food, or prayed a prayer: you built the lifeboat that kept me afloat.

To David: From the dealership days to Prestige, you have been a constant. Thank you for forgiving me years ago and showing up when it mattered most. You are one of the best friends life could bless me with.

And finally, **to you, the Reader:** Thank you for letting me share this journey with you. Whatever season you are in, whether you are climbing the mountain or walking through the valley, I pray you find the grace you need for today.

ABOUT THE AUTHOR

Jerry M. Herrin Jr. is a leader in the financial services industry, a veteran of the automotive business, and a survivor of Stage 4 renal cell carcinoma.

Jerry's career began at sixteen bagging groceries in Warner Robins, Georgia, where he learned that hard work and a crisp tie were the price of admission. He spent the next two decades climbing the ladder of the automotive world, rising from a nineteen-year-old salesperson to General Manager of a major dealership. Known for his high energy and "fixer" mentality, Jerry built a reputation for driving results, until a life-altering diagnosis forced him to redefine what success really means.

In 2019, Jerry was diagnosed with kidney cancer, which later metastasized to his lungs. Facing a prognosis with single-digit survival odds, Jerry underwent a grueling two-and-a-half-year battle involving surgery, clinical trials, and a complete physical and spiritual reset.

Today, Jerry is a passionate advocate for **Servant Leadership**, teaching others how to lead with empathy, build cultures of trust, and find "Grace in the Gaps." He believes that true leadership isn't about being the hero, but about building heroes.

Jerry lives in Georgia with his wife, Stephanie—his "General" and partner in every battle—and their two sons, Bradley and Dawson. When he isn't working or writing, you can usually find him on a golf cart at sunset, grateful for the speed of observation.

www.ingramcontent.com/pod-product-compliance
Lightning Source LLC
Chambersburg PA
CBHW030454100526
44580CB00010B/132/J